THE CHARIS PROJECT

Christian resources promoting spiritual and moral development across the curriculum

CHARIS MATHEMATICS

UNITS 10 - 19

AGE RANGE 14 - 16+

PHOTOCOPIABLE

Project Director: John Shortt
Deputy Director: Alison Farnell

THE STAPLEFORD CENTRE

First published 1997 by:
The Stapleford Centre,
Stapleford House,
Wesley Place,
Stapleford
Nottingham, NG9 8DP
Tel: 0115 939 6270
Fax: 0115 939 2076
E-mail: charis@stapleford-centre.org

ISBN 1 902234 01 4

The Charis Project is a curriculum development initiative based at The Stapleford Centre, Nottingham. Details of training courses and other publications are available from the Centre at the address given above.

The publishers are grateful to the following for permission to use the extracts and illustrations indicated:

Oxford University Press for photographs used in Unit 10 and for data derived for the table on p. 10. These all come from *The State of the World's Children 1996*, edited by Carol Bellamy and published in 1996 for UNICEF by Oxford University Press, and they are used by permission of Oxford University Press.

The London Planetarium for the illustration of the solar system by Brad Greenwood used on pages 15 and 17 in Unit 11 and page 65 in Unit 15, and published by the London Planetarium on the poster entitled *Galaxies*.

Armagh Planetarium for the illustrations of the Earth from Space, the Pleiades and the Andromeda Galaxy on pages 15, 19 and 20 of Unit 11. These were published as postcards by Armagh Planetarium.

Icon Books Ltd for quotation by Felix Pirani in Unit 11, published in *The Universe for Beginners* by Felix Pirani and Christine Roche, Icon Books, 1993.

SPCK for quotation by John Polkinghorne in Unit 11, published in *Quarks, Chaos and Christianity* by John Polkinghorne, Triangle, 1994.

Fowler Wright Books for data used in table on page 28 in Unit 12 and derived from *Teenage religion and values* by Leslie J. Francis & William K. Kay, Gracewing, 1995.

Universitätsbibliothek, Basel, Springer-Verlag GmbH & Co. KG, Heidelberg, and Stefan Hildebrandt for picture of Kepler on pages 57 and 61 in Unit 15, published in *The Parsimonious Universe* by Stefan Hildebrandt and Anthony Tromba, Springer-Verlag New York Inc., 1996.

Springer-Verlag GmbH & Co. KG, Heidelberg, and Stefan Hildebrandt for picture of Kepler's five Platonic bodies on page 63 in Unit 15, published in *The Parsimonious Universe* by Stefan Hildebrandt and Anthony Tromba, Springer-Verlag New York Inc., 1996.

Dover Publications Inc. for pictures of snowflakes on pages 61 and 67 in Unit 15, published in *Snow Crystals* by W. A. Bentley and W. J. Humphreys, Dover Publications.

Cambridge University Press for quotations by Paul Davies used in Unit 16, published in *The Accidental Universe* by Paul Davies, Cambridge University Press, 1982.

CONTENTS

FOREWORD TO THE FIRST CHARIS PUBLICATIONS BY PROFESSOR SIR STEWART SUTHERLAND

The OFSTED discussion paper of February 1994, in which I took a particular interest, *Spiritual, Moral, Social and Cultural Development*, pointed out that the development of pupils in these areas, could not be restricted to one or two periods per week and related school assemblies. The focus in question is rather a whole school and whole curriculum activity.

Schools declare and commend values under all four of these headings in a whole variety of ways - as much by what schools do as by what they teach in formal context. Equally however, there is hardly an area of the curriculum which does not, both explicitly as well as implicitly, raise questions of fundamental beliefs and values. It is this latter aspect of spiritual, moral, social and cultural development which is the concern of The Charis Project. The Stapleford Centre is to be commended for its contribution to both the debate and to classroom activity.

The Charis Project materials have the great merit of raising specific questions of beliefs and values which arise out of particular cases of subject content. This is by no means as easy as some would imply, nor would we expect the specific examples given to be uncontentious. The most important contribution of this material is to show that questions of beliefs and values do arise across the curriculum, and that to ignore that is to diminish the impact and the potential of education. There may well be differences of opinion about precisely which questions will most stimulate young minds, and which potential answers most approach adequate answers. The challenge is to enter the debate and to do so in a way that is most likely to promote spiritual, moral, social and cultural development of pupils of diverse ages and diverse backgrounds.

Stewart Sutherland
Principal and Vice-Chancellor of the University of Edinburgh
and formerly Her Majesty's Chief Inspector for Schools
May 1996

INTRODUCTION: THE CHARIS PROJECT

Teaching in the schools of the nineties

Teaching in our schools today is rather different from in previous decades. Teachers, pupils, communities and society have changed and developed, and technology has made a huge impact.

We talk of accountability and appraisal, SAT's scores and measurable outcomes, league tables and competition between schools. Somewhere, the pupil as a whole person is in danger of getting lost beneath the demands of all these outside constraints.

At the same time, the wider concerns are still there - both for legislators and for teachers. The 1988 Education Reform Act in England and Wales required schools to "promote the spiritual, moral, cultural, mental and physical development of pupils". This was further formalised by the Education (Schools) Act 1992, which saw the birth of OFSTED (the Office for Standards in Education), and of regular schools' inspections. Amongst other things, Registered Inspectors have to report on "the spiritual, moral, social and cultural development of pupils". These are not new considerations, they have always been there, but teachers are now giving more thought to this more fundamental dimension of education - the personal development of their pupils.

The development of the whole person

This renewed emphasis has spawned a mass of literature, seminars, consultations and conferences. A whole new language began to appear with much talk of the "four adjectives" or of "SMSC" (spiritual, moral, social and cultural). If that suggests that the person consists of four separate and unrelated 'bits', more recent talk of 'personal development' has re-affirmed the wholeness of the person.

The development of the whole person is clearly a whole school issue. It cannot be restricted to RE and assemblies and so become the responsibility only of those involved in these aspects of school life, of central importance though they may be. Also important to personal development, taking place as it does through personal relationships, especially those between teacher and pupil, is the ethos of the school. This pervades all aspects of the life of the school - in the classroom, in the playground, in the assembly-hall or at the bus queue.

The QCA (Qualifications and Curriculum Authority) Forum on Values in Education and the Community (1997) has emphasised the importance of considering values in all subjects of the curriculum. The QCA's school pilot guidance materials will contribute to the revision of the National Curriculum for the year 2000. It is envisaged that consideration of values should then be given much greater prominence in classroom teaching.

Promoting personal development throughout the curriculum

The OFSTED discussion paper *Spiritual, Moral, Social and Cultural Development* (February 1994) claims that the promotion of spiritual and moral development in all schools should be a whole-curriculum matter. It goes on to say that "to move to such a place where subjects see themselves in this way might seem to require a sea-change in attitudes and approaches, but certainly the potential is there".

The school, and here this means all teachers in every subject across the curriculum, is encouraged to create opportunities which:

- provide pupils with knowledge and insight into values and beliefs;
- enable them to reflect on and develop their own beliefs and values, aspects of life and experiences so that they develop spiritual awareness and self knowledge;
- encourage pupils to consider life's fundamental questions, and relate religious teaching to those questions;
- encourage pupils to explore meaning and purpose, values and beliefs;
- teach the principles which help pupils to make moral decisions and to distinguish right from wrong;
- foster values such as honesty, fairness, respect for truth, justice and property;
- encourage pupils to express moral values across issues affecting their school community;
- encourage pupils to respect other people and relate to them positively;
- encourage pupils to take responsibility, exercise initiative, participate in community and develop an understanding of citizenship;

- create opportunities to work cooperatively, and to participate cooperatively in the school community;
- teach pupils to appreciate their own cultural traditions, and the diversity and richness of others, to gain understanding of societies, families, school and communities; and
- provide opportunities to enrich pupils' cultural learning experiences.

For some teachers, the responsibility that they are now given for the personal development of their pupils could be an added burden. For others it is a welcome return to educating pupils in a more holistic manner, re-focussed away from the exam success mentality. For all teachers in every part of the curriculum, it is an opportunity to enhance their teaching styles and resources.

The Charis Project

The Charis Project was set up to produce classroom resources for teachers who are beginning to effect the sea-change in attitudes and approaches to the curriculum called for by OFSTED. The first three subject-areas tackled are English, Mathematics and Modern Foreign Languages (French and German) with Science being added subsequently. The resources have been designed with the needs of pupils aged 14 - 16 years in mind.

The teachers in the writing teams have sought to produce materials which will help their colleagues to create the opportunities set out above. In particular, they are concerned to:

- enable teachers to respond to the challenge of educating the whole person;
- help teachers to focus on the spiritual and moral dimensions inherent in their subject;
- encourage pupils towards a clearer understanding of Christian perspectives on the fundamental questions that arise in all areas of knowledge; and
- contribute to the breadth, balance and harmony of pupils' knowledge and understanding.

It is recognised that there is much that is held in common among people of various faith perspectives and of no particular religious outlook. Values are often very widely shared and there can be quite general agreement on what is true, beautiful or good. The Charis resources seek to promote these common values. At the same time, the reasons why they are held and the basic beliefs about reality in which they are grounded differ from one perspective to another. These fundamental differences lead to different total outlooks and to detailed differences on what qualities, attitudes and actions are truly moral and/or spiritual. The Charis Project is based on the belief that these differences and the distinctives of the Christian perspective are significant and that understanding this is an important element in a pupil's education and personal development and a positive preparation for life in our contemporary plural society.

We are often asked why Charis was chosen as the name of the project. We tried without success to invent a catchy acronym. The modern foreign languages teachers said we could not have an English word in the title of a French or German book so we went to Greek and Hebrew. Somebody said "charis" and we all realised how well its idea of grace and giving fitted in with one of our concerns - to provide an antidote to the consumerist "me-first" assumptions of some curriculum resources. So it became the Charis Project!

The Charis resources are offered as a starting point with ideas to help teachers to promote the personal development of their pupils while still teaching to their examination syllabus. It is also our intention that, in using these materials, teachers will be encouraged to develop their own resources and their own methodologies for the promotion of spiritual and moral development through their subject-area. In preparing them, we have experienced something of a sea-change in our own attitudes and approaches. We hope that they may stimulate our colleagues to produce more and better resources.

John Shortt and Alison Farnell
Project Directors

Introduction: Charis Mathematics

Why should mathematics teachers be concerned with spiritual and moral development?

Addressing spiritual and moral development across the curriculum has come much more to the fore recently as a result of the renewed emphasis placed upon personal development within both the National Curriculum and the OFSTED Framework for Inspection.

These facets of development are, of course, not new as goals of education. Indeed, many mathematics teachers would say that they are fundamentally concerned with the education of the "whole child". However, a shared understanding of what this means has proved to be elusive and, consequently, it has not always been seriously worked through by mathematics teachers. However, having developed these resources, the *Charis Mathematics* writers have become convinced that moral and spiritual dimensions should be and can be present in the teaching of their subject.

How can learning mathematics provide opportunities for such development?

The nature of the subject itself suggests a number of approaches for combining spiritual and moral development with the learning of mathematics.

The first of these approaches comes through recognising that mathematics has been developed and is applied in a wide range of human situations. Consequently, it is possible to choose contexts which allow students to develop their mathematics while, at the same time, reflecting upon and discussing the spiritual and moral dimensions arising from the human issues being examined. For example, Unit 9 *Could it be you?* uses the National Lottery as a context to develop probability and statistics skills. At the same time, it provides an opportunity to reflect upon what we really value and to discuss the impact, if any, of luck in our lives.

A second approach comes through recognising how people find that by exploring ideas within mathematics, they can also gain insight into broader areas. Mathematics could be seen to act as a metaphor for other areas of life. Unit 10 *Do you know where you are going?* is an example of this approach. The unit examines various aspects of the mathematics of navigation and also links this with the way we seek guidance and direction in our lives.

The third approach used in the resources comes through recognising that mathematics is used extensively to help us model and understand the universe. It is hoped that, through examining examples of this, students will develop a sense of wonder in response to the real world around them. For example, Unit 2 *The Designer Universe?* offers opportunity for students to improve skills with standard form, while reflecting on the origin and amazing nature of our universe.

What does the pack contain?

The pack consists of a set of 10 free-standing units mainly aimed at Key Stage 4 students. Some units are more appropriate for students of particular tiers, but there are some units that can be used effectively with all GCSE students. Also, during trialling, some of the units were used successfully with younger students.

Each unit contains Teacher's Notes and photocopiable Student's Sheets. The Teacher's Notes contain information on:

- the mathematical content within the unit;
- the aspects of spiritual and moral development addressed by the unit;
- background ideas and additional sources of resources;
- how the unit is structured and any special resources required; and
- how to conduct the discussion and reflection activities within the unit.

How can the units fit in with our existing scheme of work?

Teachers often express a desire to broaden the mathematical experience of their students, but feel under pressure to press on with the syllabus. The Teacher's Notes for each unit give an indication of how long the unit can take and also outline the mathematical content. Some units could either be used as a motivation for learning an area of mathematics or alternatively used to practice and apply knowledge, skills and understanding already developed.

The table shows the key mathematical content addressed by each unit and for which tiers of GCSE (Foundation, Intermediate or Higher) the unit would be suitable. The information below together with the further content details in each unit is designed to help you to identify where a unit can be usefully incorporated into your existing scheme of work.

Unit	Title	GCSE tier	Key mathematical content
10	*The literal facts*	F/I	Using fractions and percentages; working with large numbers; place value; interpreting tables; interpreting and constructing statistical diagrams.
11	*The designer universe?*	I/H	Standard form (positive powers of 10); rounding numbers to significant figures; scale drawing.
12	*Believe it or not?*	F/I/H	Data collection methods; carrying out a statistics project; using percentages.
13	*Bucking the trend*	I/H	Correlation; lines of best fit.
14	*But can you afford it?*	F/I	Understanding and calculating with percentages; sensible use of calculator.
15	*Mr Kepler's shapes*	F/I/H	Symmetry; nets and solids; construction of loci.
16	*The inside story*	I/H	Standard form (positive/negative powers of 10); substitution in formulae.
17	*What's the time?*	F/I/H	Complex calculations, negative numbers; large numbers; using formulae; constructing graphs; calculating means.
18	*Could it be you?*	F/I/H	Calculating probability; interpreting tables; carrying out and interpreting surveys; combinations and factorials; number patterns.
19	*Do you know where you are going?*	F/I	Compass points; bearings; scale drawing

What preparation will I need to do?

Having decided when you want to use the unit with your students, we recommend that you study the Teacher's Notes closely. After this you will need to:

- consider whether and how you will teach the students any relevant mathematics prior to work on the unit;
- photocopy the Student's Sheets and organise any other necessary resources;
- plan how to structure the unit over a series of lessons;
- consider the implications for classroom organisation; and
- allow time for any preliminary activities with the students (units 3 and 9).

What if I am not used to teaching mathematics in this way?

Many teachers may be hesitant about organising lessons that stimulate discussion of issues not normally addressed during mathematics lessons. Also, students may initially find the experience strange if they have not done similar work in the past. However, it was found when trialling the materials that if the approach was appropriately introduced then students enjoyed engaging with the spiritual and moral dimension and that stimulating discussion did take place.

Guidance is given in each unit about possible areas for discussion and reflection. It is helpful to ask students to produce written responses prior to a class or group discussion of an issue. It is also important to realise that your role is not to provide answers but to enable students to think through the spiritual and moral issues raised by the unit.

Given the innovative nature of these resources, the project team would appreciate any feedback from teachers on their experience of using the materials. There is a form at the end of the book which you can use if you wish to respond, or you may prefer to send a letter/fax/e-mail. We trust that the resources will support you as you seek to promote both the personal and mathematical development of your students.

John Westwell and John Shortt
Editors of Charis Mathematics

The literal facts

UNIT 10

In this unit, students analyse international statistical data on population, literacy and education. They also reflect upon their own educational experience and contrast it with that of others around the world.

Using this unit

The unit is designed primarily for students at the Foundation/ Intermediate Tier of GCSE and should last for about 3 hours.

It is intended that the unit be used to consolidate students' knowledge and understanding of Number and Data Handling work rather than to introduce new work.

It looks at 9 different countries from around the world. Students use and analyse information on population, literacy, primary and secondary school enrolment and average national income. Students are encouraged to think about their own situation and to compare it to countries that may be "worse off".

The students are encouraged to consider their own educational opportunities contrasting these with children in the other countries covered. This should provoke reflection and discussion, which are both important elements of the unit.

In parts of the unit, what it means for someone to be illiterate is addressed. Consequently, if the class contains students with learning difficulties or particularly poor reading skills then extra sensitivity may be required.

Students will require a ruler, calculator and graph paper (task 3). A world atlas would also be helpful.

Mathematical content

Number (AT2)

- Ordering numbers, showing an understanding of place value
- Working with large numbers (millions/billions)
- Rounding numbers to the nearest whole number
- Finding and expressing approximate proportions using simple fractions and percentages
- Expressing one number as a percentage of another

Handling Data (AT4)

- Extracting and interpreting information from tables
- Interpreting pie charts and bar charts and drawing conclusions
- Introduction to correlation

Spiritual and moral development

The aim of this unit is to help students to appreciate the value of the education they receive. They are also encouraged to imagine what life must be like for other children around the world.

TEACHER'S NOTES

Background

UNICEF was founded in 1946 in the aftermath of the Second World War as the United Nations International Children's Emergency Fund. Each year it publishes a report on 'The State Of The World's Children' which contains many statistics and also analysis and comment. The figures used in this unit come from the 1996 report.

In 1990 the United Nations organised the World Summit for Children at which almost all the world's governments agreed goals for achievement in 1995 and 2000. These cover infant mortality, disease, sanitation and malnutrition as well as the educational goal featured in the unit.

Additional sources

1. *The state of the world's children* published for UNICEF by Oxford University Press is available from UNICEF, Unit 1, Rignals Lane, Chelmsford, Essex, CM2 8TU. (01245) 476315
2. *Summing Up the world* published by Development Education in Dorset, available from DEED, Kingsleigh School, Hadow Road, Bournemouth, BH10 5HS. (01202) 532484

Notes on the activities

Throughout the unit there are places where students are encouraged to stop and reflect. When planning the lessons, it is important that time is allowed for class or group discussion. Students can then be encouraged to talk about their thoughts and be ready to listen to others who may well have different opinions.

It is suggested that the International Data sheet is copied onto a separate sheet of paper to help the students to make use of it in the various sections.

Literacy

Task 1 would be best done as a weekend homework prior to starting the unit properly.

Before working on the countries' data, it may be worthwhile for the students to find out where in the world the countries are. Some students may have trouble interpreting the table of data and so it is recommended that each of the categories be explained at an early stage.

Class discussion

The section on literacy raises a large number of issues that could be the basis for class discussion. It is important to build on the work students have been doing and so it is worth while discussing:

- how different their weekends were without any reading or writing;
- whether they were surprised by the amount of illiteracy in some countries;
- the alternative forms of communication used by people.

Going to school

This section examines the proportion of children, boys and girls, that attend school in different countries. The data used here is called the enrolment ratio - the number of children engaged in schooling at that level expressed as a percentage of the total number of children of the relevant ages.

In this section, students should be encouraged to reflect on the significant differences between countries. In thinking about what else children may be doing, the students might offer answers such as working to help support their families or even involvement in war.

School children

This section examines the proportions of the different countries' populations that are children of school age. It also encourages the students to examine links between these proportion figures and literacy rates.

Class discussion

After the sections on *going to school* and *school children* the class could discuss:

- whether they were surprised by the variation in school attendance around the world;
- the different opportunities for boys and girls;
- what children are doing if they are not at school.

Measuring success

This section examines the average national income in each of the countries. It also encourages students to consider what the best measure of the success of a country might be. Students might suggest education, literacy, infant mortality, crime rate.

Conclusion

In this final section students are encouraged to see how progress can be made and is being made in education in some parts of the world.

Class discussion

It would be good for the unit to conclude with a final discussion summarising and drawing together the issues raised. The students could discuss:

- how realistic the goal set by the World Summit for Children is;
- whether the goal is too limited and a higher target should be set;
- what governments should be doing to work towards the goal;
- how what they have learnt in the unit affects their views about their own education.

Extension activity

Students could be asked to do research into other information about the 9 countries (e.g. life expectancy, infant mortality, debt, health facilities). Some more extensive work on correlation could then follow.

Alternatively, students could pick a country of their own choice (maybe a country with which they have some sort of an association) and find out its comparable figures. They could then compare their findings.

Answers

Task 2:

1. a) 5,760,000,000. b) 1,100,000,000.
   c) Approximately $^1/_5$. d) Approximately 1 in 5 people in the world cannot read or write a simple sentence.

2. a) Niger (12%), Burkina Faso (17%), Ethiopia (31%), Haiti (41%), India (48%), Rwanda (55%), Philippines (94%), UK (97%), USA (99%).
   b) 8th (or the 2nd highest country).
   c) 88%. d) 88 people. e) 3%. f) 3 people.

Task 3:

1.

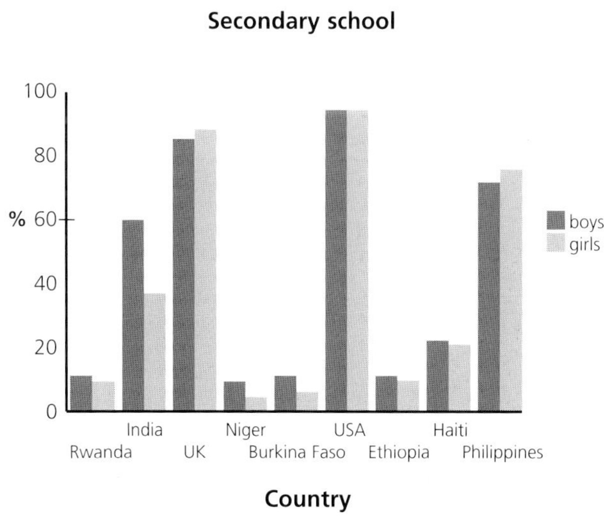

2. a) UK and USA; high literacy.
   b) Niger and Burkina Faso; low literacy.
   c) Boys; variety of answers.
   d) India.

3.

	Boys	Girls
Rwanda	89	91
India	40	63
UK	15	12
Niger	91	96
Burkina Faso	89	94
USA	6	6
Ethiopia	89	90
Haiti	78	79
Philippines	29	25

Task 4:

1. Rwanda 2,400,000; India 227,900,000; UK 8,100,000; Niger 2,700,000; Burkina Faso 2,900,000; USA 40,700,000; Ethiopia 15,600,000; Haiti 1,900,000; Philippines 17,800,000.
2. Rwanda 31%, India 25%, UK 14%, Niger 30%, Burkina Faso 29%, USA 16%, Ethiopia 29%, Haiti 27%, Philippines 27%.
3. a) Rwanda and Niger.
   b) UK and USA.
   c) High literacy.
   d) Low literacy.
   e) Countries with higher percentages aged between 5 and 16 are often poorer, so there is less finance for education and more pressure on girls to have children early.

Task 5:

1. a) UK and USA; high GNP.
   b) Niger and Burkina Faso; low GNP.
   c) (i) £1008.33.
      (ii) £232.69.
      (iii) £33.15.
   d) (i) £15 (Niger); £16.67 (Burkina Faso).
      (ii) £3.46 (Niger); £3.85 (Burkina Faso).
      (iii) £0.49 (Niger); £0.55 (Burkina Faso).
   e) 5 to 6 days.

The literal facts

UNIT 10

We all go to school in this country because we have no choice! However, we can sometimes take it for granted that we are able to go to school. In this unit we will be looking at how many people in various countries are literate as well as at how many have the opportunity to go to school. You will be using information about 9 countries given in the table of international data provided.

Literacy

Most of us learned to read and write a long time ago. However, there are many people in the world who are less fortunate than us.

For many children there is little or no opportunity to learn to read and write.

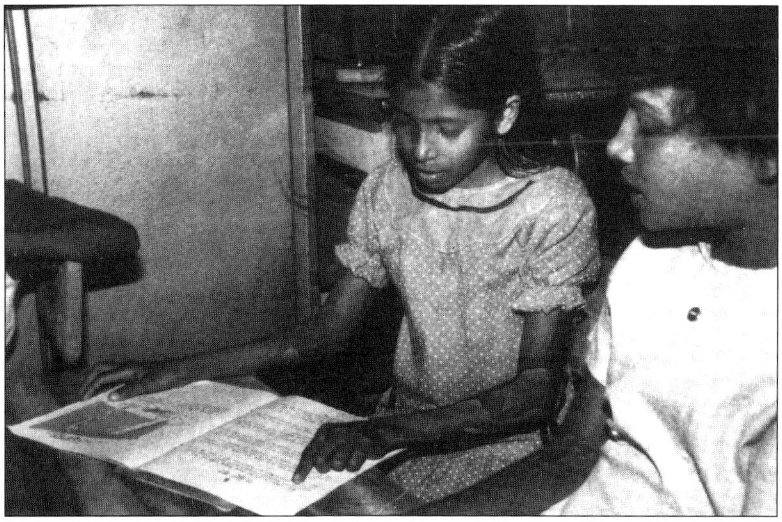

1

1. Imagine you do not know how to read or write.
   Think how this would affect a weekend at home.
   Consider, and write down, all the things that you would not be able to do, things that normally you would take for granted.

2. What jobs could you do if you did not know how to read or write?

info

Literate - A person who can read and write a simple sentence.

Illiterate - A person who cannot read and write a simple sentence.

Read the definitions.

Are you literate or illiterate?

2

1. a) The population of the whole world is estimated to be 5.76 billion. Write this number out in full in figures (1 billion is equal to 1000 million).

b) It is estimated that there are 1.1 billion people in the world who are illiterate (that is, they cannot read and write even a simple sentence). Write this number out in full.

c) Using the pie chart to help you, estimate what fraction of the world cannot read and write a simple sentence.

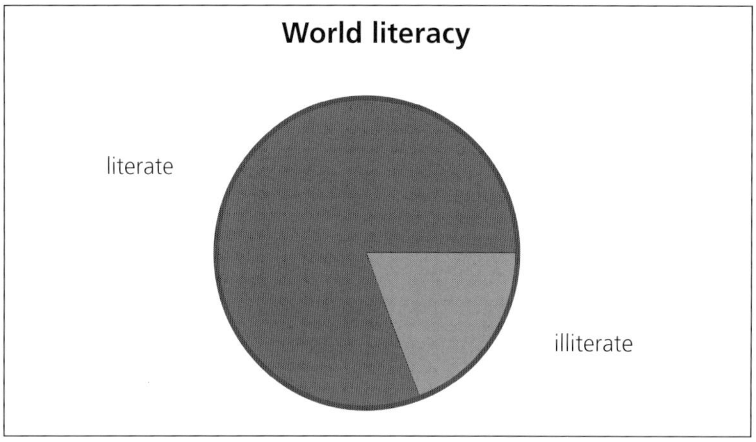

d) Using your previous answer, copy and complete the following sentence.
Approximately 1 in ___ people in the world cannot read and write a simple sentence.

Does it surprise you that such a large proportion of the world's population cannot read and write?

2. a) Using the adult literacy figures for 1990 from the International Data table, rank the countries in order starting with the country with the lowest adult literacy rate (that is the smallest percentage of people aged 15 or over who can read and write).

b) Where does the UK come in the list?

c) The country with the lowest adult literacy rate in the world is Niger with 12%. This means that only 12% of the adult population of Niger can read and write a simple sentence. What percentage of Niger's adult population is illiterate?

d) Copy and complete this sentence (remember % means "out of 100"):
In Niger, about ____ adults in every 100 cannot read and write a simple sentence.

e) What percentage of the adult population of Britain are illiterate?

f) Copy and complete this sentence:
In Britain, about ____ adults in every 100 cannot read and write a simple sentence.

What other ways do you think people use to communicate?

Going to school

Most people learn how to read and write when they are at school. In countries like Britain, almost everyone goes to a primary and a secondary school. There are, however, many countries where the story is very different.

3

1. This bar chart shows the percentage of boys and girls at secondary school for each country. Copy and complete the bar chart using the figures given in the main table. Use a scale of 1 cm for every 10% on the vertical axis.

Secondary school

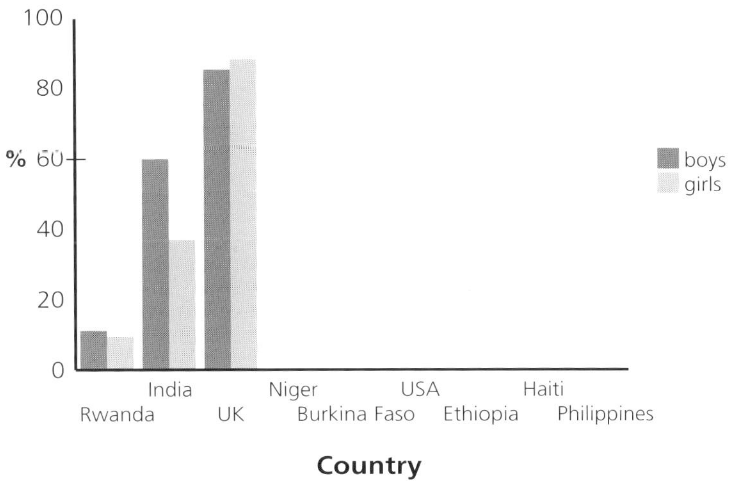

2. Use the bar chart to help you to answer the following questions:
   a) Write down the names of the 2 countries with the highest secondary school figures. Do these countries generally have high or low literacy rates?
   b) Write down the names of the 2 countries with the lowest secondary school figures. What do you notice about the literacy rates of these countries?
   c) In most countries, do more of the boys or more of the girls go to secondary school? Does this surprise you? What do you think might be the reasons for this?
   d) For which countries is the difference between boys and girls largest?

3. Copy and complete this table to show the percentage of boys and girls who do not go to a secondary school. The first country has been done for you.

% not at secondary school

	Rwanda	India	UK	Niger	Burkina Faso	USA	Ethiopia	Haiti	Philippines
Boys	89								
Girls	91								

In some countries many children are not at school. What do you think they are doing instead?

School children

When we think of school children, we normally think of those aged between 5 and 16. Some countries have a large proportion of their population within this age group. For other countries the proportion is quite small. We are going to work out, for each of the countries, the percentage of the population aged between 5 and 16 years old.

4

1. Use the information on population to copy and complete the table on the right. To work out how many children there are in each country aged between 5 and 16, you have to subtract the number of children under 5 from the number of children under 16. The first one has been done for you.

3.8 million - 1.4 million = 2.4 million = 2,400,000

Country	Number of children aged between 5 and 16
Rwanda	2,400,000
India	
UK	
Niger	
Burkina Faso	
USA	
Ethiopia	
Haiti	
Philippines	

2. We are now going to work out, for each country, the percentage of the total population that is aged between 5 and 16. You need to do the following calculation for each country:

$$\frac{\text{Number of children aged between 5 and 16}}{\text{Total population}} \times 100$$

Copy and complete the table below rounding off your answer to the nearest whole number.
Using your calculator, check that you agree with the answer for Rwanda.

$$\frac{2.4}{7.8} \times 100 = 31\% \text{ (to nearest whole number)}$$

3. a) Write down the names of the 2 countries with the largest percentage of their population aged between 5 and 16.
   b) Write down the names of the 2 countries with the smallest percentage of their population aged between 5 and 16.
   c) Do countries with a small percentage of their population aged between 5 and 16 generally have high or low literacy rates?
   d) Do countries with a large percentage of their population aged between 5 and 16 generally have high or low literacy rates?
   e) Why do you think the above is generally true?
   You may wish to discuss these findings with your teacher.

Country	Percentage of total population aged between 5 and 16
Rwanda	31%
India	
UK	
Niger	
Burkina Faso	
USA	
Ethiopia	
Haiti	
Philippines	

Measuring success

The GNP (Gross National Product) of a country is a way of measuring the wealth of that country. It is often used to determine how successful a country is.

Are there other things apart from wealth that could be used to show how successful a country is?

5

1. a) Find the 2 countries with the highest adult literacy rate. What do you notice about the GNP of these 2 countries compared with other countries?

   b) Find the 2 countries with the lowest adult literacy rate. What do you notice about the GNP of these 2 countries?

c) The GNP figure tells you the income of an average person in a year. The GNP figure for the UK is £12,100.
   (i) Calculate the average monthly income of a person in the UK.
   (ii) Calculate the average weekly income of a person in the UK. (There are 52 weeks in a year.)
   (iii) Calculate the average daily income of a person in the UK. (There are 365 days in a year.)

d) Choose one of the countries you mentioned in part b). Calculate the average income for a person in that country for:
   (i) a month
   (ii) a week
   (iii) a day.

e) Roughly how many days would you have to work in the UK in order to earn the same as someone earns in a whole year in the country you chose in part d)?

Conclusion

There has been much work done over the last fifty years to promote the needs of children around the world. Organisations such as UNICEF are working hard to bring about better opportunities for children.
For example, in 1970 in most countries, less than 40% of girls had access to any real sort of education. Now nearly 70% of girls around the world can receive some sort of an education.
In 1990, the World Summit for Children took place. A number of goals to be achieved by the year 2000 were agreed by almost all of the world's governments. One of the goals was to provide:
"Basic education for all children and completion of primary education by at least 80% of children - girls as well as boys."

Using the information on primary school completion found in the main table, do you think this is a realistic target?

How do you think governments and countries, including our own, can help to achieve this goal?

Living in this country we all have the opportunity to go to school and have a decent education. Yet we can so often take this for granted. Many children around the world do not have even the most basic education. There are other things that we are also fortunate to have compared to others, whose lives are full of insecurity. For example, many children around the world have limited health care, little in the way of food and live under the constant threat of war.

How has this unit changed your views about the education you receive?

International Data

Here is a table showing information about nine different countries around the world. The information comes mainly from a report produced by UNICEF called "The State of the World's Children". UNICEF is the United Nations International Children's Emergency Fund.

Country	Area (square km)	Total population (millions) 1995	Population under 16 (millions) 1995	Population under 5 (millions) 1995	Adult literacy rate (%) 1970	Adult literacy rate (%) 1990	Primary school completion (%) 1993	Secondary school (%) 1993 Boys	Girls	GNP/capita (£ pounds) 1993
Rwanda	26,000	7.8	3.8	1.4	34	55	59	11	9	140
India	3,204,000	918.6	344.5	116.6	33	48	62	60	37	200
UK	244,000	58.1	12.0	3.9	97	97	99	85	88	12,100
Niger	1,267,000	8.9	4.5	1.8	5	12	82	9	4	180
Burkina Faso	274,000	10.1	4.7	1.8	5	17	70	11	6	200
USA	9,373,000	260.6	60.9	20.2	99	99	99	94	94	16,580
Ethiopia	1,222,000	53.4	25.9	10.3	5	31	22	11	10	70
Haiti	28,000	7.0	3.0	1.1	23	41	47	22	21	250
Philippines	300,000	66.2	27.0	9.2	83	94	75	71	75	570

Adult literacy rate: The percentage of people aged 15 or over who can read and write.
Primary school completion: The percentage of children who complete primary school.
Secondary school: The percentage of boys (B) and girls (G) of secondary school age who go to school.
GNP/capita: Average annual income per person.

The designer universe?

UNIT 11

In this unit, the Universe provides a context for students to work with numbers expressed in standard form using positive powers of ten. They also consider some of the amazing facts that scientists are discovering about Earth's place within the Universe.

Mathematical content

Number (AT2)
- Rounding numbers to a given number of significant figures
- Standard form (with positive powers of ten only)
- Multiplying of powers of numbers

Shape and Space (AT3)
- Scale drawing

Spiritual and moral development

The unit aims to promote a sense of wonder about the Universe and also to encourage students to reflect on the possibility of the Universe being designed.

Using this unit

The unit is intended for students at the Intermediate/Higher Tier of GCSE. The focus of the work is on numbers written in standard form, but only positive powers of 10 are used. There is only a brief note on standard form in the text, so students will need to have been taught how to write numbers greater then ten in standard form before they attempt the unit. (Negative powers are addressed in the unit, "The Inside Story".) It is expected that the unit will last for about 2 to $2\frac{1}{2}$ hours.

The unit has several sections, each looking at different aspects of the Universe and offering an interesting context within which standard form can be practised. There is also opportunity for discussion about our place in the Universe and reflection on issues related to the Anthropic Principle. Students are asked to consider different points of view and make up their own minds.

There is an extension activity at the end for more able students.

Students will need A3 paper (task 3, question 3), a calculator, compasses and a ruler.

Background

In recent years, there has been a growth of interest in popular science writing. Some of these books report how scientists, who have studied the place of Earth in the Universe, have been amazed and challenged by the precision and balance they have found. There appear to be so many variables that are "just right" for the production of the conditions necessary for life on Earth. This has led many to conclude that the Universe was designed in order to produce such life. This is known as the 'Strong Anthropic Principle'. Some scientists respond to this purposeful design by searching for a loving, creator God. Others, Stephen Hawking amongst them, will only subscribe to a weaker form of the principle and argue that, if conditions were not suitable for life, we would not be here discussing them!

Additional sources

Books:
P. C. W. Davies, *The Accidental Universe* (Cambridge University Press, 1982).
John Polkinghorne, *Quarks, Chaos and Christianity* (Triangle, 1994).
Felix Pirani and Christine Roche, *The Universe for Beginners* (Icon Books Ltd., 1993).
Michael Poole, *A Guide to Science and Belief* (Lion, 1994).
Christopher Maynard, *Stars and Planets* in the Usborne Young Scientist Series (Usborne, 1991).
Philip & Phylis Morrison, *Powers of Ten* from the office of Charles and Ray Eames (Scientific American Library, 1982).
Further Science from the "Science at Work" series (Longman, 1993).
David Wilkinson, *God, the big bang and Stephen Hawking* (Monarch, 1993).

Video:
"Powers of Ten" the film, produced by the office of Charles and Ray Eames. Available on video cassette (ISBN 0-7167-5029-5) from Marketing Dept., W. H. Freeman and Company, 41 Madison Avenue, New York, NY 10010.

Internet:
Internet pictures from the Hubble telescope at http://www.seds.org/hst/hst.html

Notes on the activities

The unit requires an introductory activity in order to start students thinking about their place in the Universe. Task 1 could be used for this purpose. However there are alternative resources suggested in the additional sources section. The video or the book *Powers of Ten* would be a powerful introduction, as would a selection of pictures from the Hubble telescope. Some students may belong to an astronomy club and could be asked to give a short presentation.

Earth and its moon

The students are given a definition of standard form in the text, but it is important that students have been introduced to writing numbers in standard form. They also need to know how to round numbers to a given number of significant figures before beginning this section.

TEACHER'S NOTES

Our solar system

Question 3 within task 3 is a drawing exercise, so equipment and paper is needed at this stage.

Class discussion

This section leads students into considering the two sides of the Anthropic Principle argument and is an opportunity for a class debate. It is important, therefore, that when planning lessons, time for class/group discussion is included. The issues that could be addressed are:

- their understanding of the argument put by Pirani;
- their understanding of the argument put by Polkinghorne;
- their own opinions on the two arguments and their own reactions to the conditions for life being "just right".

Students could be asked to prepare short talks supporting one side of the argument or the other.

The Milky Way

This section requires students to multiply numbers given in standard form, for which they may need support. Before this section, scientific calculators are not necessary. However, from this stage onwards the students can practise using the standard form function on the calculator. Some students may need support in this.

The Universe

This is the final core section and again leads students into reflecting on the origins of the Universe.

Class discussion

It is recommended that students make a written response to the text. This helps prepare them for a concluding discussion on the ideas raised by the unit. This might address:

- their reactions to the immense size of the Universe;
- whether they think that life came about through amazing chance or through design;
- whether their views on these issues affect the way they live their lives.

Light years away (extension activity)

This activity offers more challenging problems.

Answers

Task 1:

Jo Planet, 15 Nowhere Street, Rotherham, South Yorkshire, England, United Kingdom, The British Isles, Europe, The Northern Hemisphere, Earth, The Solar System, The Milky Way, The Galaxies, The Universe.

Task 2:

1. 1.2756×10^4 km.
2. a) not possible to be so accurate over such a large distance.
   b) 40,100 km.
   c) 4.01×10^4 km.
3. a) 3.476×10^3 km.
   b) 1.09×10^4 km.
4. a) 3.84×10^5 km.
   b) 7.68×10^5 km.

Task 3:

1. Mercury 4.878×10^3; Venus 1.21×10^4; Earth 1.2756×10^4; Mars 6.79×10^3; Jupiter 1.428×10^5; Saturn 1.2×10^5; Uranus 5.24×10^4; Neptune 5.045×10^4; Pluto 2.3×10^3.
2. Pluto; Mercury; Mars; Venus; Earth; Neptune; Uranus; Saturn; Jupiter.
3. Scale drawing.
4. Mercury 57,900,000; Venus 108,000,000; Earth 149,600,000; Mars 227,900,000; Jupiter 778,000,000; Saturn 1,427,000,000; Uranus 2,870,000,000; Neptune 4,497,000,000; Pluto 5,900,000,000.
5. Saturn.
6. Pluto.

Task 5:

1. 2×10^{51} kg.
2. 4.4×10^6 km.
3. 7.6×10^{23} tonnes.
4. 1.1×10^{21} tonnes.
5. 2.5×10^8 years.

Task 6:

1. a) 8.4×10^8 km.
   b) 2.6×10^9 km.
2. 4×10^{51} kg.

TEACHER'S NOTES

Task 7 (Extension):

1. a) 1.8×10^7 km.
   b) 1.08×10^9 km.
   c) 2.592×10^{10} km.
   d) 9.4608×10^{12} km.
   e) 9.46×10^{12} km.
2. 2.2×10^{19} km.
3. 3.0×10^{17} km.
4. 1.2×10^{18} km.
5. 2.5×10^{17} km.
6. a) 3.8×10^8 km.
   b) 7.8×10^7 km.
   c) 3.6×10^4 km per hour.
   d) 30 days.
   e) Mars and Earth will move relative to each other during the journey and so the spacecraft will have to travel along a curved path.

TEACHER'S NOTES

The designer universe?

UNIT 11

In this unit you will be working with large numbers written in standard form. The Universe provides us with plenty of examples of very large numbers. But before we get going, let's think about where we are in the Universe.

1 Have you ever sent a letter to someone and tried to make their address as long as possible? Here is a list of some of the places you could use to write to someone called Jo Planet who lives in the town of Rotherham.

The Northern Hemisphere; 15 Nowhere Street; The Solar System; Jo Planet; The Universe; Earth; The British Isles; England; Rotherham; The Galaxies; Europe; United Kingdom; South Yorkshire; The Milky Way.

Write Jo Planet's address in the correct order.

To a cosmologist (someone who studies the Universe) there is nothing remarkable about our Earth.

It is just a small planet with one moon ...

circling an ordinary star, the Sun.

The Sun is a medium sized star in a galaxy, the Milky Way.

There are thousands of millions of galaxies in the Universe.

But, there is one very extraordinary thing about planet Earth ...
... we live here!!!

info

Distances in space are enormous and so it is best to write any numbers in standard form.

Remember, a standard (or scientific) form number comes in three parts:

- A number between 1 and 10 (not including 10 itself)
- A multiplication sign
- A power of 10

For example 3.67×10^{11}

Earth and its moon

Now let's take a closer look at our amazing Universe.

2

1. Earth has a diameter of 12,756 km. Write this number in standard form.

2. We can now calculate the distance around the equator by using the formula for the circumference of a circle.

Circumference of the Earth $= \pi \times$ diameter of the Earth
$= \pi \times 12756$
$= 40{,}074.15589$ km

This is the answer you might get on your calculator but it is not sensible to give the answer to this degree of accuracy.

a) Write a sentence explaining why it is sensible to round off this number.
b) Write the answer accurate to 3 significant figures.
c) Write your answer to part b) in standard form.

3. The diameter of the Moon is approximately one quarter of the diameter of the Earth. The Moon's diameter is 3,476 km.

a) Write this number in standard form.
b) Calculate the circumference of the moon giving your answer in standard form to three significant figures.

4. The Moon is, on average, about 384,000km from the Earth.
a) Write this distance in standard form.
b) If a spacecraft travels to the Moon and back again, approximately how far has it travelled? Give your answer in standard form.

Our solar system

Our Earth is just one of nine planets which circle round the Sun. Here are their vital statistics starting with the planet nearest to the Sun.

Planet	Diameter (km)	Planet	Diameter (km)
Mercury	4,878	Saturn	120,000
Venus	12,100	Uranus	52,400
Earth	12,756	Neptune	50,450
Mars	6,790	Pluto	2,300
Jupiter	142,800		

3

1. The diameter of the Earth can be written in standard form as 1.2756×10^4 km. Copy the list of planets above and write each of their diameters in standard form.

2. List the planets in order of size, starting with the smallest.

3. To get an idea of how the planets' sizes compare, you are now going to do a scale drawing on A3 paper. You need to draw circles for each of the planets. It is a good idea to draw Jupiter in a corner first and then Saturn. The radii for the circles are as follows: Mercury, 0.35cm; Venus, 0.85cm; Earth, 0.90cm; Mars, 0.50cm; Jupiter, 10cm; Saturn, 8.40cm; Uranus, 3.65cm; Neptune, 3.50cm and Pluto, 0.15cm.

   You can see that Earth is a rather small planet but it does have some great advantages over the others. To see what these are we will look at some more "planet statistics".

Planet	Average distance from Sun in km	Planet	Average distance from Sun in km
Mercury	5.79×10^7	Saturn	1.427×10^9
Venus	1.08×10^8	Uranus	2.87×10^9
Earth	1.496×10^8	Neptune	4.497×10^9
Mars	2.279×10^8	Pluto	5.9×10^9
Jupiter	7.78×10^8		

4. Mercury is, on average, 57,900,000 km from the Sun. Copy the list of planets and write their average distances from the Sun in full in the normal way.

5. Which planet is approximately ten times as far away from the Sun as Earth?

6. Which planet is approximately one hundred times as far away from the Sun as Mercury?

The outer planets, Jupiter, Saturn, Uranus, Neptune and Pluto, are a long way from the Sun and so are very cold. The temperature in the cloud layers on Neptune has been estimated to be -220°C. **So Earth's first advantage is its distance from the Sun.**

The inner planets are Mercury, Venus, Earth and Mars. These are closer to the Sun but all except Earth are barren, rocky places with little or no water. Approximately 71% of the Earth's surface is covered in water. All life depends on the presence of water.
So Earth's second advantage is the presence of water.

Mars and Mercury have little or no atmosphere and so suffer extremes of temperature too great for living things. Venus and Earth each have atmospheres which act like blankets and keep the planet temperatures steady. However, the mix of gases in the atmosphere on Venus causes a super-greenhouse effect. Venus suffers from temperatures of about 500°C!
So Earth's third advantage is its atmosphere.

4

Are we just lucky to have the right conditions for life on Earth? Some scientists think so ...

We are the way we are because the universe is the way it is ... and not vice versa.
Felix Pirani

Others believe the opposite ...

... it's not just 'any old world', but it's special and finely tuned for life because it is the creation of a Creator who wills that it should be so.
John Polkinghorne

Science cannot prove or disprove these statements. They are statements of personal belief. We all make up our own minds what to believe once we have looked at the different points of view.

Write a short summary of the two sides of the argument above. Discuss your ideas with a friend or with the class.

The Milky Way

Let us now look a bit further into our remarkable Universe.

Our Sun is a medium-sized star in our galaxy, the Milky Way. On a clear night you can see the Milky Way stretched out across the sky like a dim trail of light. No one knows how many stars it contains, one estimate is 10^{12}. So the mass of the Milky Way is estimated to be about the mass of the Sun multiplied by 10^{12}.

5

Give all your answers in standard form.

1. If the mass of the Sun is 1.989×10^{39} kg, use the information given above to calculate the approximate mass of the Milky Way. Give your answer to 1 significant figure.
2. The diameter of the Sun is 1.4×10^{6} km. Calculate the circumference of the Sun. Give your answer to 2 significant figures.
3. The Sun converts 1.26×10^{14} tonnes of hydrogen into energy every year. If it has enough hydrogen left for another 6×10^{9} years, how many tonnes of hydrogen does it contain? Give your answer to 2 significant figures.
4. Using the data in question 3, calculate the number of tonnes of hydrogen that the Sun will use up in the next 9 million years. Give your answer to 2 significant figures.
5. It takes the Sun approximately 250×10^{6} years to move around the centre of our galaxy. Write this number in standard form.

The Universe

Our galaxy, the Milky Way, is just one amongst many scattered like dust throughout the vastness of the Universe. Each galaxy is a swirling pool of millions of stars.

6

For the following questions, give all your answers in standard form.

1. The star, Betelgeuse, is part of the constellation Orion. Betelgeuse has a diameter approximately 600 times the diameter of our Sun. Our Sun has a diameter of 1.4×10^6 km.
   Giving your answers to 2 significant figures, calculate:

   a) the diameter of the star Betelgeuse;
   b) the circumference of the star Betelgeuse.

2. The Andromeda galaxy is twice as massive as the Milky Way. The Milky Way is about 10^{12} times the mass of the Sun. If the Sun has a mass of about 2×10^{39} kg, calculate the approximate mass of the Andromeda galaxy.

All scientists agree that the scale and complexity of the Universe make it truly awesome. Some believe that it has all come about as a matter of chance, but others believe that they have found too many "coincidences" in the delicate balance of conditions throughout the history of the Universe. It has been said that the probability of life emerging within the Universe "by chance" is about the same as the probability of a tornado blowing through a scrap-yard and producing a jumbo jet!

What do you think?

Light years away

Distances in deep space are so vast that they are measured in light years.
Light travels faster than anything else at a speed of 3×10^5 km per second.

7

1. Giving all your answers in standard form, how far does light travel
   a) in one minute?
   b) in one hour?
   c) in one day?
   d) in a year of 365 days?
   e) round your answer to d) to 3 significant figures.

   Your answer to part e) is a **distance** but it is called **one light year**. Check this answer with your teacher before going on to the remaining questions.)

In each of the following questions, give your answers to 2 significant figures.

2. The Andromeda galaxy is the most distant object we can see with the naked eye.
   It is 2.3×10^6 light years away from Earth.
   How far away is Andromeda in km?

3. At its widest point, the Milky Way is approximately 3.2×10^4 light years across.
   How far is this in km?

4. The approximate length of the Milky Way is 1.3×10^5 light years.
   How far is this in km?

5. Our Sun is approximately 2.6×10^4 light years from the centre of the Milky Way.
   How far is this in km?

6. a) If the Earth is 1.496×10^8 km from the Sun and Mars is 2.279×10^8 km from the Sun, how far is it from Earth to Mars when all three are in a straight line with the Sun between Earth and Mars? Give your answer in km and in standard form.

   b) Use your calculator to repeat part a) when all three are in a straight line with Earth between the Sun and Mars. Give your answer in standard form.

   c) When Earth and Mars are in the position described in part b), a spacecraft travels from Earth to Mars. If the spacecraft were able to travel in a straight line, how fast would it have to travel in order to complete the journey in three months? Assume that Mars and Earth do not move further apart during the journey, and that each month has 30 days. Give your answer in km per hour.

   d) In fact, the spacecraft can travel at 1.1×10^5 km per hour.
   How many days will it take to cover the distance? Give your answer to the nearest day.

   e) Give a reason why, in reality, the spacecraft in part d) would actually take longer to reach Mars.

Believe it or not?

UNIT 12

This unit helps students to learn about methods of collecting data and the impact that different approaches can have on the results. At the same time, they will reflect on their own beliefs and learn more about their peers' beliefs.

Using this unit

This unit could be used with students of any tier at GCSE as an introduction to different methods of collecting data. It could be particularly helpful as preparation for GCSE coursework which involves handling data. The unit lasts between 2 and 4 hours depending on the time given over to the students' own research.

In the unit, students are surveyed about their beliefs, using three different methods of data collection. Once the data has been processed, the students examine the impact that the different methods have on the results produced.

A second activity allows them to analyse and interpret the results of a national survey in this field. They also compare the national figures with those of their class. In the final activity, students carry out an independent piece of statistical research thus developing their data handling and report writing skills.

Throughout the unit, it is important to encourage respect for the beliefs of others and sensitivity to the possibility of their reluctace to talk about them.

Students need a calculator, protractor and ruler.
Students would also benefit from using a computer spreadsheet package such as Excel.

Mathematical content

Number (AT2)
- Finding one number as a percentage of another

Handling Data (AT4)
- Designing, using and evaluating methods of collecting data including straw polls, interviews and questionnaires
- Representing data using appropriate diagrams, including bar charts, pie charts and scatter diagrams
- Interpreting data including comparing sets of data and evaluating the reliability of results

Spiritual and moral development

The aim of this unit is to help students to become more aware of both their own and others' beliefs. At the same time, it is hoped they will become more sensitive to other students' views.

Background

Statistical research is regularly carried out into the beliefs and opinions of the population. Sometimes the results produced can be surprising, particularly in the area of religious belief. This can raise questions as to how the results were produced and particularly how the data was collected.

The unit allows students to make comparisons with national figures for England and Wales produced by the Francis and Kay research at Trinity College, Camarthen. In the course of their work, just over 13,000 year 9 and 10 students were surveyed in 1994. The students were given a substantial questionnaire and invited to complete it anonymously and confidentially during school time. The survey did not deal with faiths other than Christianity.

Additional sources

L. J. Francis and W. K. Kay, *Teenage Religion and Values* (Gracewing, 1995)

Notes on the activities

Throughout the unit, there are opportunities for students to discuss their beliefs formally and informally. As this is one of the objectives of the unit, such discussion must not be seen as a distraction from the mathematics.

Tell me what you believe

There are two stages to this activity and they need to take place in different lessons to allow time for the data to be processed.

Preliminary stage (30 minutes)

In the preliminary stage, students are asked to respond to three different data collection methods all addressing the same issues. It is important to explain to students that they may be surprised by some of the questions in the survey, but that they are essential for the work that follows. Some may feel that the questions are personal, but explain to them that this sort of difficulty is one of the issues addressed by the unit. The first method is the anonymous questionnaire (worksheet provided). This questionnaire sheet is all that the students should have at this stage and it should be completed in exam conditions. As the sheet is given out, it is important to stress to students both the confidentiality and anonymity of this first approach.

After collection of the completed questionnaires, the students need to get into pairs for the second method, the one-to-one interviews. It is important to stress that these are private and only the interviewer and yourself will know their responses. Initially, it is best to give out just one copy of the interview sheet (worksheet provided) to each pair. When one of them has finished an interview then a second sheet can be issued.

The final method is a straw poll. You should ask the students to respond to the 10 statements. A straw poll record sheet is provided. In each case they should say whether they agree, are not certain or disagree. Here you should insist that they do respond and that you have the correct total for each statement. This should be done as a whole class activity with the students putting up their hands appropriately.

Note that until the data has been processed (a class results *pro forma* is provided), it is not possible to continue with 'Tell me what you believe'. It is possible, however, to start students thinking about task 3, their personal research projects.

Stage 2

In the second stage, the students should receive a copy

of the class results and the student sheets. They should read the introduction and then do the questions in task 1 which can be done individually or as a group. However, all students should record their answers so they can be referred to during a whole class discussion.

Class discussion

When students have completed the questions it would then be appropriate for the whole class to discuss the following:

- the differences which they noticed resulting from the three different methods;
- why they think those differences occurred;
- what they think are the advantages and disadvantages of each method;
- why people are sometimes reluctant to talk about their beliefs.

What does everyone else believe?

In this activity, students analyse and interpret the data provided by the Francis and Kay survey of teenage religion and values and compare it with their class results. In task 2 the students practise data representation and interpretation skills including working with pie charts, bar charts and scatter diagrams. Some students may need some revision on these prior to beginning the task. The activity also has the potential to be supported by the use of a spreadsheet in analysing and presenting the data.

Class discussion

Once students have completed task 2, it would then be appropriate for the class to discuss:

- the key differences which they noticed between the national and class surveys;
- how they account for these differences;
- why any national results particularly surprised them.

Personal research project

In this final activity, the students carry out their own survey and write a report on the results. This can be an individual or group activity and could be used to assess AT1 criteria. Guidance is offered in the student's sheet, but there may well be need to offer more structure to some students. In particular, the practicalities of collecting the data may need to be discussed with the class.

Once the reports are finished, there is scope for them to be presented to the whole class and for discussion on the reliability of the research.

Answers

Task 1:

2. Differences may occur because of mistakes made in the data collection process or because of the reluctance of people to reveal personal beliefs.

3. a) Anonymous questionnaire:
   advantages - anonymity;
   disadvantages - possible misunderstanding of the information required.
   b) Interview:
   advantages - confidentiality, questions can be clarified;
   disadvantages - cost.
   c) Straw poll:
   advantages - speed of gathering information;
   disadvantages - no confidentiality.

Task 2:

2. a)

I believe in God - % nationally

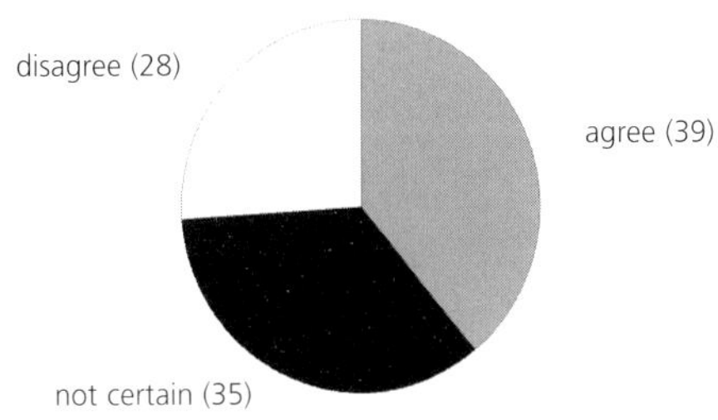

b)

I believe in ghosts - % nationally

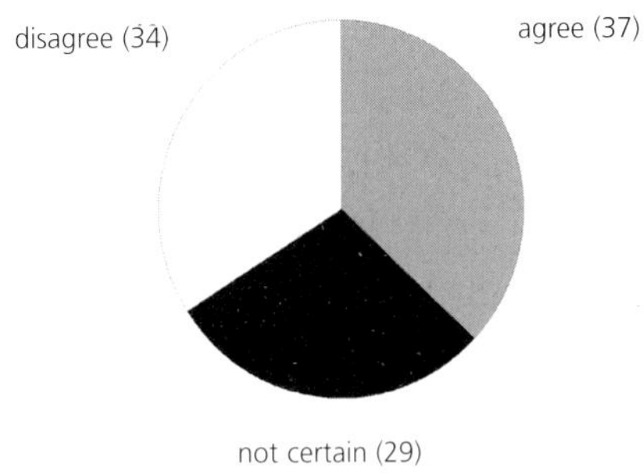

4. Possible example

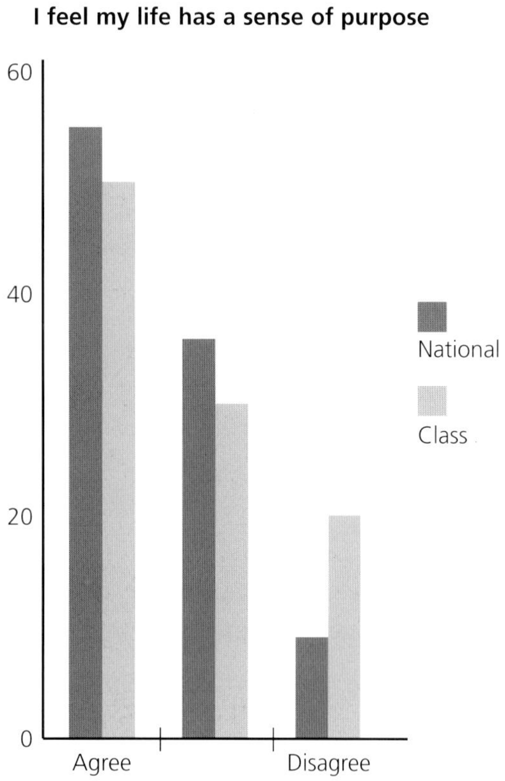

7. This is a large sample for a national survey and so results can be generalised with some confidence.

Believe it or not?

UNIT 12

Do you know what your beliefs are?

Do you know what your friends believe? Do they know what you believe? Would you want them to?

Is it difficult to talk to other people about what you believe? If so, why?

During this unit, you will be learning some statistical techniques, but also spending time thinking about some of the issues above.

Tell me what you believe

There are many ways to collect information about people's beliefs and opinions. You have already used three of the most important approaches. They are:

Anonymous questionnaires
First you filled in the questionnaire. This was confidential so nobody knows what your responses were.

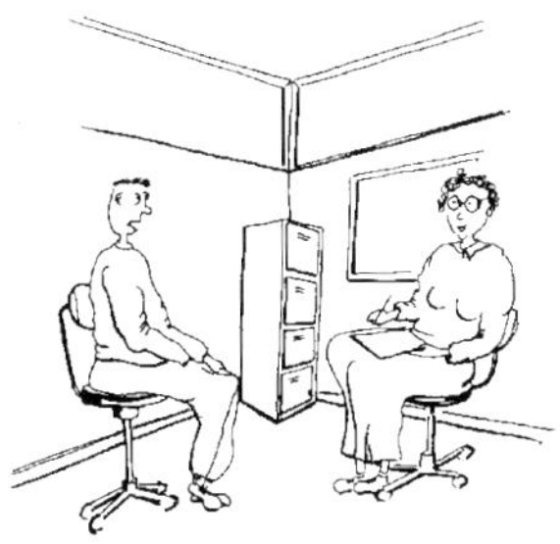

Private interviews
For this method, you worked in pairs. You each used an interview sheet. You took it in turns to be an interviewer. The results of the interview should only be known by the pair of you and your teacher.

Straw Polls
In this case, your teacher read you the 10 statements. For each one you had to say if you agreed, were not certain or disagreed. You had to do this publicly and at the same time as everyone else.

1

Now you can analyse the results as your teacher has processed the data. Using your class results, answer the following questions.

1. Write down any differences you notice between the results given by the three different methods.
2. Write down why you think there are these differences.
3. Write down the advantages and disadvantages of each of the three data collection methods.
4. Which method do you think is most reliable for collecting the data in this particular case? Explain why.
5. Are there any class results from the anonymous questionnaire which are different from what you would have expected? Write down which ones.

What does everyone else believe?

In 1994 researchers carried out a major survey into teenage religion and values. Over 13,000 year 9 and 10 students in England and Wales completed anonymous questionnaires. As well as covering topics including religious beliefs and the supernatural, the survey also addressed issues of right and wrong, sexual morality and substance use. The results for the statements that you have already been working on are shown below.

The national picture

Statement	Agree	Not certain	Disagree
I believe in God	39%	35%	26%
I feel my life has a sense of purpose	55%	36%	9%
I believe in life after death	41%	41%	18%
I believe God punishes people who do wrong	19%	39%	42%
I believe in my horoscope	35%	31%	34%
The bible seems irrelevant to life today	30%	43%	27%
I believe Jesus Christ really rose from the dead	30%	43%	27%
I believe in ghosts	37%	29%	34%
I often feel depressed	53%	18%	29%
The church seems irrelevant to life today	27%	46%	27%

2

1. Complete a table like the one for the national survey, but this time for your class results. You only need to do this for your class' anonymous questionnaire results - agree, not certain, disagree. You will need to convert the numbers of students to percentages (given to the nearest whole number).

2. For each of the statements below, draw two pie charts, one illustrating the national picture and the other illustrating your class results. The pie charts should have three sections, agree, not certain and disagree.
   a) I believe in God
   b) I believe in ghosts

3. For each of the statements in question 2, look at the national pie charts and the class pie charts. What differences do you notice between the national picture and the class picture.

4. For each of the statements below, draw a single bar chart that allows the national and class picture to be compared. In each case the bar chart should include the percentage agreeing, not certain and disagreeing.
   a) I feel my life has a sense of purpose
   b) I often feel depressed
   c) I believe in life after death

5. For each of the statements in question 4, point out any important differences between your class results and the country as a whole.

6. For this question you only need to use the percentages that agreed with the statements in the national and class surveys. Draw a scatter diagram as shown in the example. In the case shown, 55% in the national survey agreed with the statement "I believe my life has a sense of purpose" while only 45% agreed in the class. You have to plot points in this way for each of the statements.

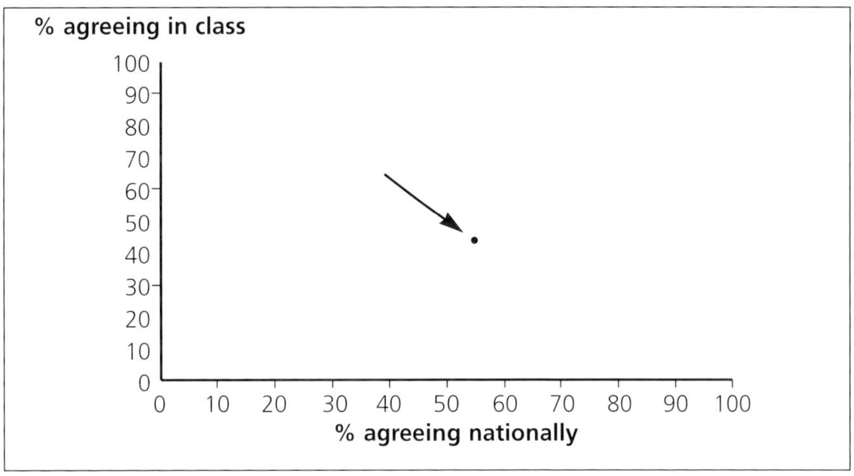

   Describe the correlation, if any, between the two sets of data.

7. Over 13,000 students were surveyed to produce the national picture results. That is only about 1.5% of all the year 9 and 10 students in the country during that year. Do you think this was a big enough sample of students to get a reliable idea of the national picture?

8. Write down any results in the national survey which were particularly different from what you would have expected. Explain why.

3

Personal research project

In this activity, you will carry out your own research into beliefs or opinions. You will then write a report describing what you did and what you found out.

Stage 1

You must first decide what beliefs you are going to investigate and predict what results you think you might get. (In your report, make clear any hypothesis you had at this stage before you started the research.)

Stage 2

You must then decide how you will collect the data and how large a sample you will survey. You must then collect the data. (In your report, explain why you decided on your particular collection method and include an example of it.)

Stage 3

Having collected the data, you must process it and represent it using tables and appropriate diagrams. (In your report, only use diagrams that you think are relevant.)

Stage 4

Finally, you must interpret the results and compare them with what you originally predicted. (In your report, make clear whether you think your research has proved or disproved your hypothesis or has left you needing to do more research.)

Teacher's record sheet for use during straw poll

Statement	Agree	Not certain	Disagree
I believe in God			
I feel my life has a sense of purpose			
I believe in life after death			
I believe God punishes people who do wrong			
I believe in my horoscope			
The bible seems irrelevant to life today			
I believe Jesus Christ really rose from the dead			
I believe in ghosts			
I often feel depressed			
The church seems irrelevant to life today			

Class Results Pro Forma for collating the results from the three methods

Statement	Agreed			Not certain			Disagreed		
	A.Q.	P.I.	S.P.	A.Q.	P.I.	S.P.	A.Q.	P.I.	S.P.
I believe in God									
I feel my life has a sense of purpose									
I believe in life after death									
I believe God punishes people who do wrong									
I believe in my horoscope									
The bible seems irrelevant to life today									
I believe Jesus Christ really rose from the dead									
I believe in ghosts									
I often feel depressed									
The church seems irrelevant to life today									

Interview sheet

Instructions for the interviewer:

1. Make sure you interview the person privately.
2. You must not tell other people what you find out during the interview.
3. You are the one who records the results. Do this by ticking the appropriate box.
4. You may need to repeat the statements.
5. Remember to record the person's name.
6. When you have finished give the sheet to the teacher.

The interview

Begin the interview by saying "I am going to read some statements. For each one, I want you to say whether you agree with, are not certain about, or disagree with the statement from your own point of view. Do you understand?"

Name: ______________________________

Statement	Agree	Not certain	Disagree
I believe in God			
I feel my life has a sense of purpose			
I believe in life after death			
I believe God punishes people who do wrong			
I believe in my horoscope			
The bible seems irrelevant to life today			
I believe Jesus Christ really rose from the dead			
I believe in ghosts			
I often feel depressed			
The church seems irrelevant to life today			

Anonymous questionnaire

Instructions :

1. Make sure you fill in the questionnaire without anyone seeing.
2. You must not write your name on the sheet.
3. Read each of the statements. In each case, say whether you agree with, are not certain about or disagree with the statement. You are answering from your own point of view.
4. When you have finished, fold the sheet once and give it to the teacher.

Statement	Agree	Not certain	Disagree
I believe in God			
I feel my life has a sense of purpose			
I believe in life after death			
I believe God punishes people who do wrong			
I believe in my horoscope			
The bible seems irrelevant to life today			
I believe Jesus Christ really rose from the dead			
I believe in ghosts			
I often feel depressed			
The church seems irrelevant to life today			

Bucking the trend

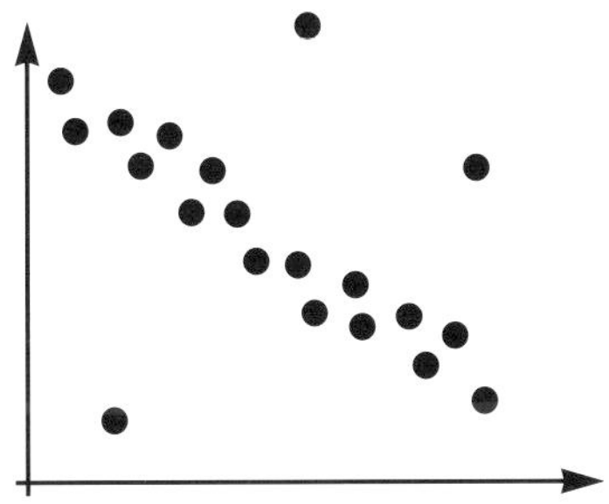

UNIT 13

This unit deals with scatter diagrams and correlation. It explores the relationship between correlation and cause, and whether behaviour is necessarily determined when there is a known correlation.

Using this unit

The unit is designed for students at Intermediate and Higher Tiers of GCSE and will last for about 3 hours. The unit could be either used to introduce scatter diagrams and correlation or as revision. The students need basic graphical skills and the ability to use algebraic formulae.

Students begin by looking at scatter diagrams and lines of best fit. Then the concept of correlation is introduced. The relation between correlation and causality is considered next. The unit introduces Spearman's correlation coefficient, as an example of a numerical measure of correlation. The unit ends with a discussion of how far behaviour can be explained, or excused, by correlation - should we "follow a trend"?

There is a small extension section on non-linear correlation.

Access to spreadsheets such as Excel would help students in this work.

Mathematical content

Handling Data (AT4)

- Scatter diagrams and lines of best fit
- The concept of correlation
- Spearman's rank order correlation coefficient

Spiritual and moral development

The aim of this unit is to encourage students to think about whether behaviour can ever be justified just because it is in line with a trend and to consider to what extent a trend may remove their personal responsibility. It is also hoped that they will reflect on whether rather intangible characteristics such as happiness can be measured.

TEACHER'S NOTES

Notes on the activities

It happens all the time

This is an introductory activity and could be addressed through a whole class discussion. At this stage, there is no need to discuss the validity of the statements, but instead just ensure meaning is clear. Discussion could focus on the seemingly less quantifiable categories such as happiness and success and how they might be measured.

Scatter diagrams and Line of best fit

These two sections introduce the ideas of scatter diagrams and lines of best fit. There are both explanations and practice examples. Students could work individually.

More data may be required for further practice. One way of getting a good quantity of data that offers possible correlation is to ask each member of the class to bring in a sheet with a number of their own details on it. These could include height, hand-span, shoe size, house number etc. This provides a source for a great number of scatter diagrams, and, eventually, correlation coefficients. It should be asked for as part of a homework assignment, in preparation for the lesson itself.

Correlation or cause?

This section addresses the interpretation of situations where correlation occurs. The connection between correlation and cause is a complex idea and students may need support.

Class discussion

It is worth bringing the class together to discuss their answers, including:

- which statements they think are true and why;
- for the true statements, whether one factor causes another or there is third factor.

Correlation coefficients

Although correlation coefficients do not appear in most GCSE syllabuses, it is worth introducing students to the idea that correlation can be quantified. Indeed, students may already have met correlation coefficients in Geography or Science (particularly Biology) and so it is worth consulting with these departments about the topic.

Spearman's rank order is chosen partly due to its accessibility. It should be noted that no explanation is given regarding tied ranks.

Will you buck the trend?

It is preferable that the whole class should work on this section at the same time. If some students have finished earlier work, they could try the extension activity - *Don't overdo it!* - before starting this section. The final core section encourages students to question what happens when there are genuine trends. In particular, is it necessary to follow the trend? Some of the examples within the section should be used sensitively, as they may well apply to members of the class, and there is a danger of a reinforcement of a negative self-image. The point is that it is possible to avoid the trend.

Class discussion

The students' responses to this final section would inform a productive class discussion and issues addressed could be:

- whether they agree with the new examples given in question 2;
- whether they know of real exceptions to genuine trends;
- whether they think there is pressure to follow trends in society.

Don't overdo it! (extension activity)

This final section is an extension task which contains examples of trends which are not linear.

Answers

Task 1 and Task 2 (question 1):

1.

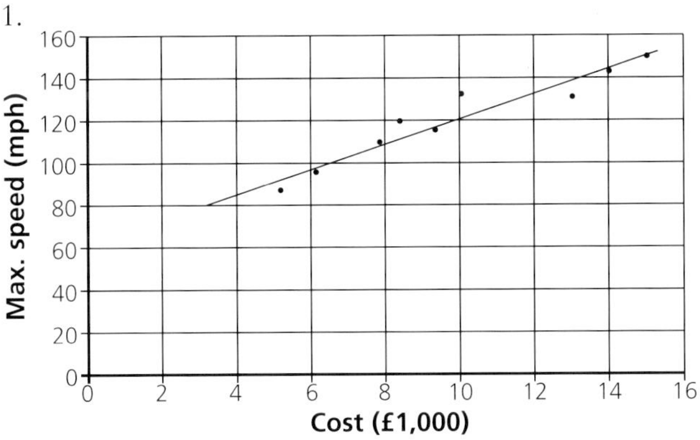

2.

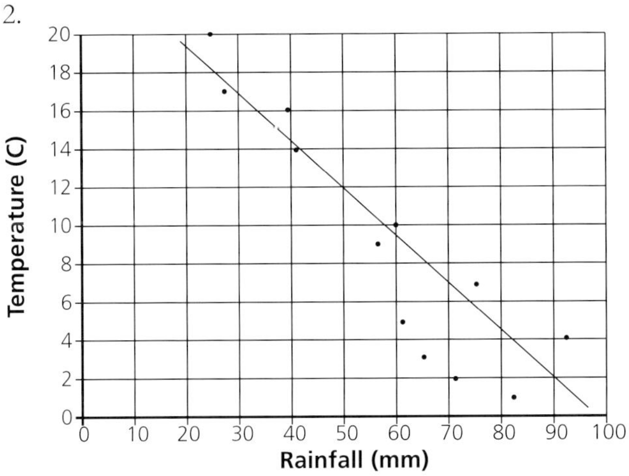

3.

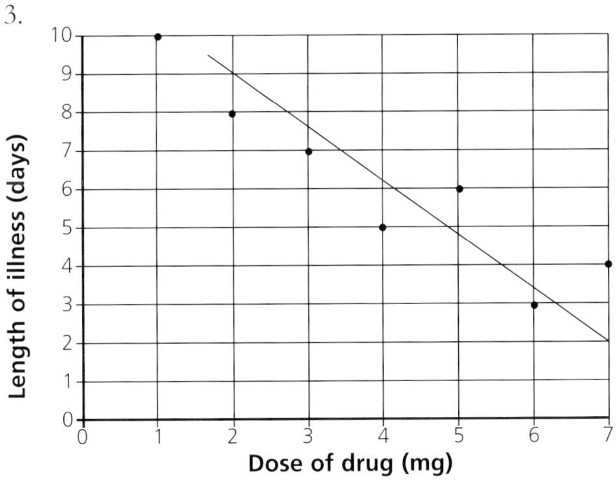

Task 2:

2. a) 130 mph.
   b) 58 mm.

3. a) possibly about 2 days (uncertain due to extrapolation).
   b) extrapolation gives meaningless answer.

Task 3:
Discussion.

Task 4:
1. r = 1, positive correlation.
2. r = -1, negative correlation.
3. r = 19/21 = 0.905, positive correlation.
4. r = 29/30 = 0.997, positive correlation.
5. r = -128/143 = -0.895, negative correlation.
6. r = -13/14 = -0.929, negative correlation.

Task 5:
Class discussion. There are a number of successful dyslexics e.g. Susan Hampshire (actress), Michael Heseltine (politician). Duncan Goodhew (swimmer) and Ian Botham (cricketer) both had asthma.

Task 6:
All three examples show non-linear correlation, where a straight line would be inappropriate, but where there is still evidence of a trend. In all three cases, too much of one quantity produces a decrease in the second.

1. a)

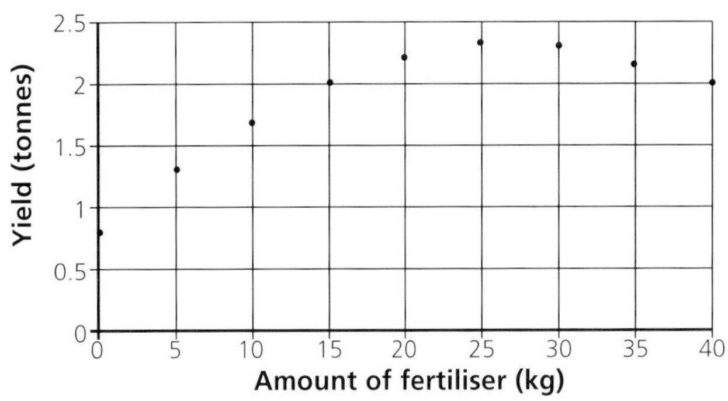

b) No.
c) Non-linear.
d) Too much fertiliser can damage the crop.

2. a)

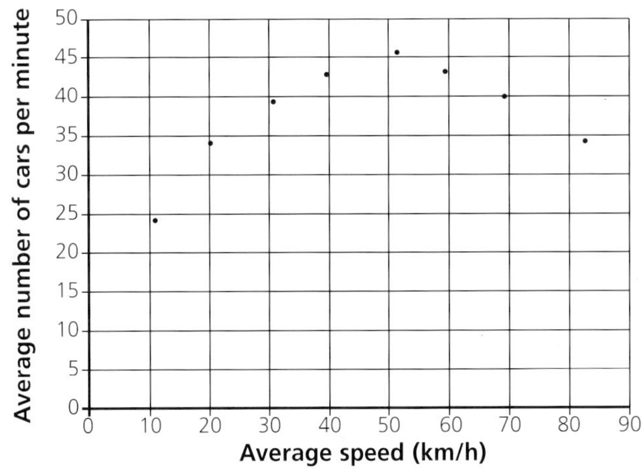

b) Low speeds probably occur during congestion when traffic moves very slowly and high speeds when there is little traffic and it is well spread out.

c) Non-linear.

3. a)

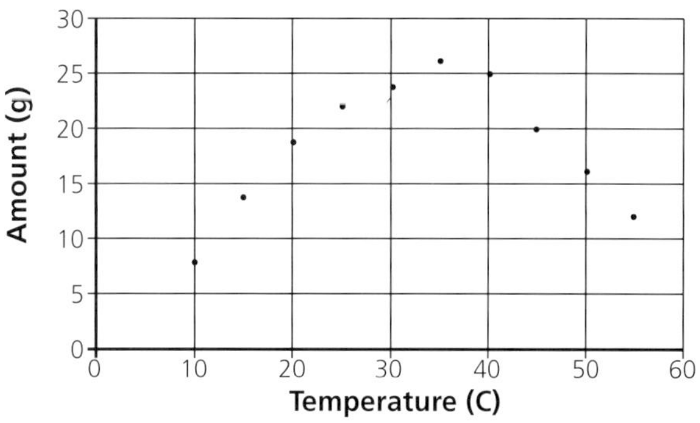

b) When temperature gets too hot growth is damaged, when it is too cold growth cannot start.

c) Non-linear.

Bucking the trend

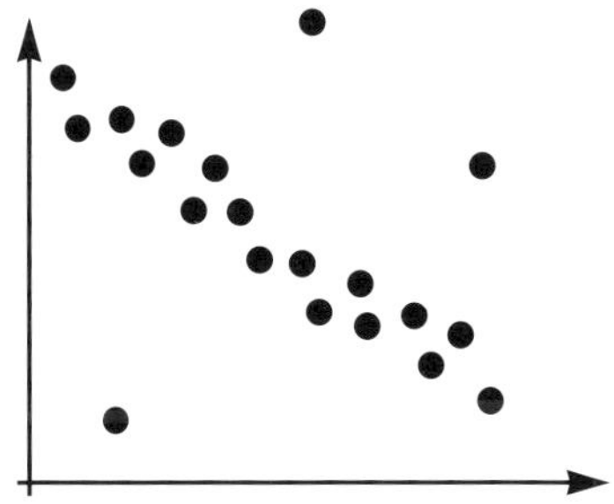

UNIT 13

It happens all the time!

Here are some statements which may or may not be true. In each one it is claimed that one aspect of a person's (or team's) character or behaviour suggests a second one will also be the case. What do you think?

- The taller you are, the faster you run.
- The better you are at Maths, the worse you are at French.
- The more money you earn, the happier you are.
- The more goals a team scores, the higher up the League it will be.
- The more you smoke, the shorter your life will be.
- The cleverer you are, the more money you will earn.
- The better a boy is at sport, the more girl-friends he will have.
- The more you pray, the more successful you become.
- The more a car costs, the higher its top speed is.
- The harder you work, the better GCSE results you get.
- The more Vitamin C you take, the fewer colds you get.
- The further away you live from school, the longer it takes to get there.

Scatter diagrams

We are now going to look at the first two statements in more detail. To do this, we would actually need some data. For example, for the first statement above, we would need data on heights and running speeds for a number of people. Some possible results are shown in the table.

Person	John	Fred	Ann	Chris	Sally	Bill	Lisa	Sarah
Height (m)	1.6	1.9	1.7	1.8	1.5	1.4	1.3	1.1
Speed (m/s)	4.8	7.2	6.4	5.8	2.8	4.6	3.4	1.6

Can you see that, in general, there is a tendency for the taller people to have faster speeds? However, this is not always true – compare, for example, the speeds of Sally and Bill. It is quite difficult, in fact, to see what is really going on by just listing the data numerically. As is often the case, it is very helpful to draw a graph. We need to use a scatter diagram.

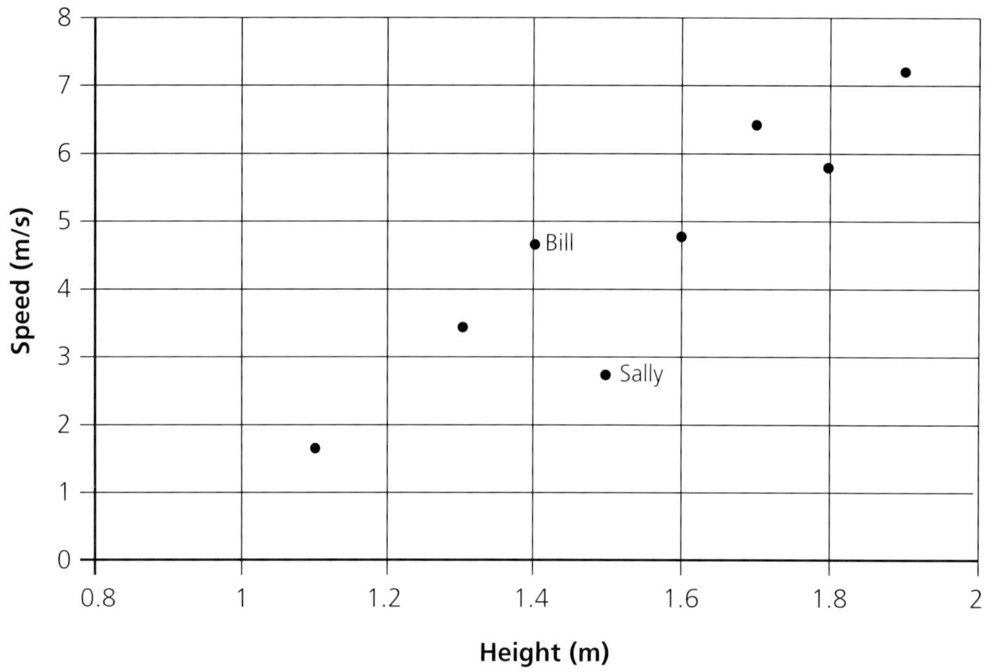

In this graph, each person is shown as one point, and we plot the two measurements for each person, their height and their speed, using the two axes. The graph shows much more clearly that for these people there is a general trend, the taller the people are the faster they run. We call this trend **correlation**. The graph also shows more clearly the people who do not follow the trend.

Next let us look at a table of results and a scatter diagram linked to the second statement. The results of some pupils in two tests, French and Maths, are shown.

Pupil	A	B	C	D	E	F	G	H	I	J
French	23	45	67	34	78	26	75	56	36	58
Maths	67	35	26	50	22	75	20	46	47	36

Again, there is a fairly definite trend, but it is different from the first example. In this case, as one feature gets bigger, the other one gets smaller. This is called negative correlation, in contrast to the previous case, which was positive correlation.

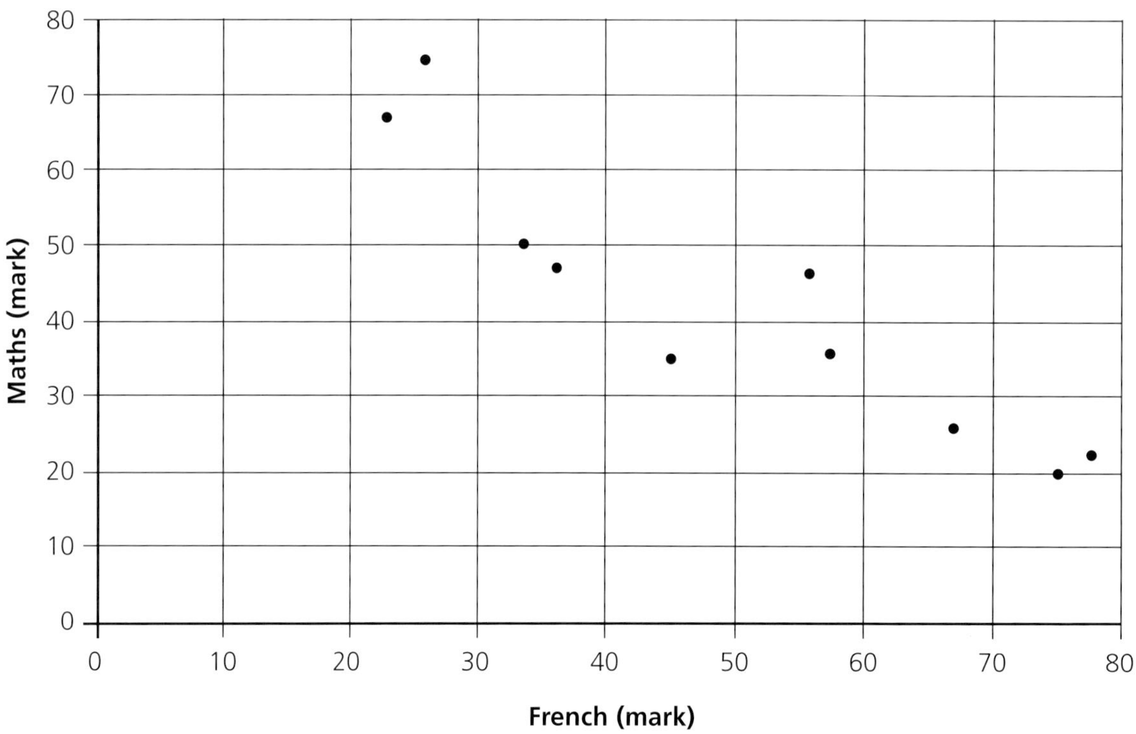

1

Plot scatter diagrams for the following sets of data. In each case write down whether there is any correlation between the data; if there is, say whether it is positive or negative.

1.

Type of car	A	B	C	D	E	F	G	H	I
Cost of car (£1000)	5.1	6.2	7.8	8.4	9.3	10.1	12.9	14.0	14.9
Top speed (m.p.h.)	86	95	110	120	115	132	131	144	150

2.

Month	J	F	M	A	M	J	J	A	S	O	N	D
Rainfall (mm)	71	82	93	75	60	41	27	24	39	56	61	65
Monthly temp. (°C.)	2	1	4	7	10	14	17	20	16	9	5	3

3.

Patient	A	B	C	D	E	F	G
Dosage of drug (mg)	1	2	3	4	5	6	7
Length of illness (days)	10	8	7	5	6	3	4

Line of best fit

Where there is a clear trend, it can be useful to illustrate this by drawing a straight line through the data. Although there are some fairly complicated rules about finding precisely the right line, it is often good enough just to use your common sense in drawing it. One useful guide is to aim to have as many of the points below the line as above it. Here is how a best straight line for the first set of data might look.

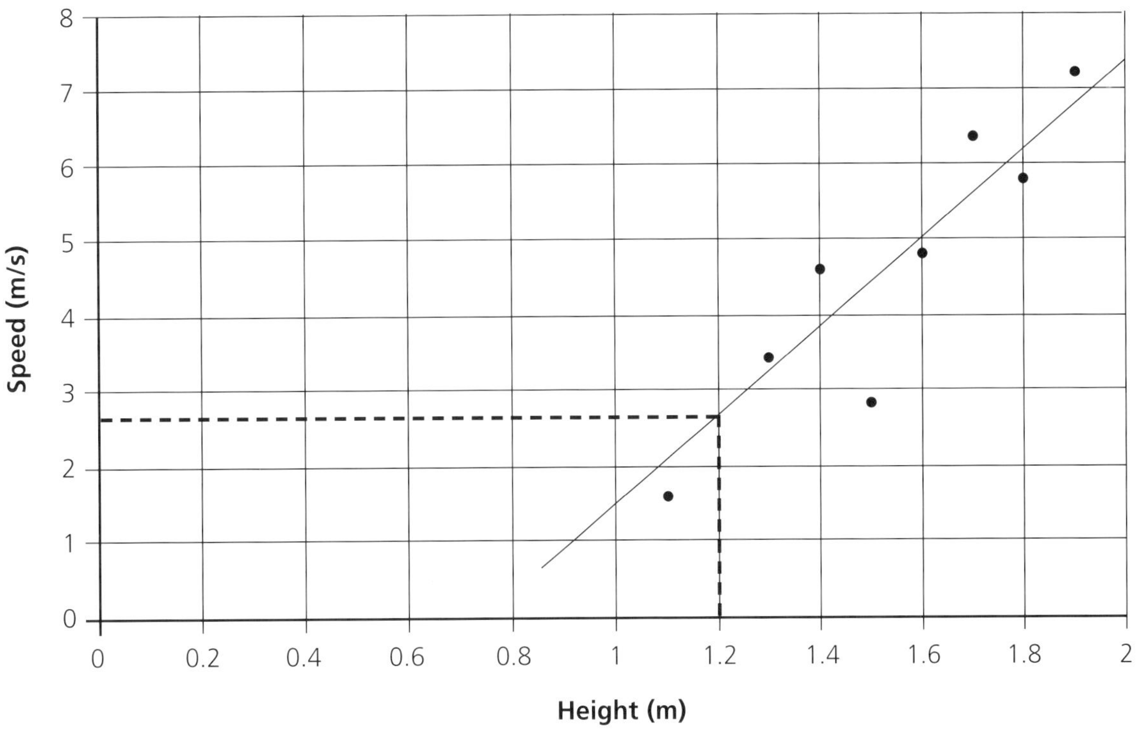

Lines of best fit can be used to estimate new values. In the athletics example, we might wonder how fast someone who is 1.2 m tall might run. By reading up to the line of best fit and across, we can see that 1.2 m corresponds to 2.7 m/s, and so that would be our estimate of the person's speed.

2

1. Go back to the scatter diagrams you did in Task 1. Draw a line of best fit on each one. Make sure that it gives a good sense of the way the data is going.

2. Use the appropriate lines of best fit from question 1 to answer the following questions.
   a) A new car costs £10,900. Estimate its top speed.
   b) A meteorologist loses the rainfall records for March. Knowing that the temp is 10°C, what should she estimate the rainfall as?

3. It is usually safe to use the line of best fit to fill in gaps between points (interpolation), but it can be unwise to use it to find values beyond the original data (extrapolation). Use the line of best fit from the medical case to estimate:
   a) How long would the illness be if 9mg of drug was given?
   b) How long would the illness be if 20 mg of the drug was given? Is this sensible?!

Correlation or cause?

Very often, two sets of data are correlated because one causes the other. Tall people are generally faster runners because their height helps them. People good at Maths are generally good at Physics because their mathematical skill helps in their Physics.

However, there are other situations where the characteristics are not directly related, but which both depend on a third item. For example, in the last ten years, there has been a positive correlation between the number of dishwashers bought each year and the number of video cameras bought each year. No-one would suggest, however, that buying a dishwasher creates an urge in a person to buy a video camera! Instead, both things have happened because better technology has made the items more available and cheaper, and increased earnings have enabled more people to buy them.

3

Look again at the statements you read at the beginning of the unit.

1. Which of these do you think are true?

2. For those which you think are true, which do you think occur because
   a) one factor causes the other (try to explain why) or
   b) because they are both caused by a common third factor (try to say what)?

So correlation does not necessarily mean that one factor is causing another. We cannot put responsibility - credit or blame - onto one item, just because it is correlated with something else. For example, the trend in the second last statement might not prove that Vitamin C actually prevents colds. It might just be that people who bother to take Vitamin C are very health-conscious people anyway, who look after themselves in all sorts of ways, and so stay healthy. Use of Vitamin C could just be a reflection of their behaviour, not a cause of their health.

Correlation coefficients

When a scatter diagram contains a large number of points, it can be difficult to judge whether or not there really is any correlation. One person might think that there is evidence of a trend, another might disagree. To help sort out these problems, statisticians have developed a way to produce a number as a measure of the correlation.

This number is called the correlation coefficient and ranges between -1 and +1. For perfect positive correlation the coefficient is +1 and for perfect negative correlation it is -1. Most situations, of course, give something in between -1 and +1. If, for example, we get a coefficient of 0.8, then that suggests that there is a quite strong positive correlation, even though it is not perfect.

Correlation of +1

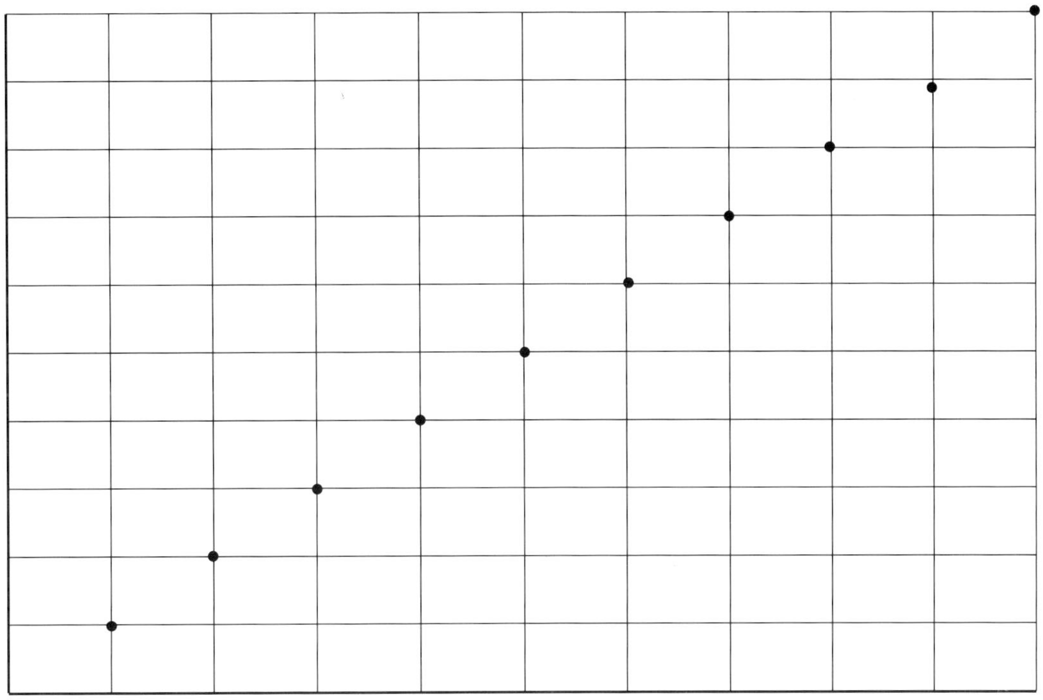

Correlation of -1

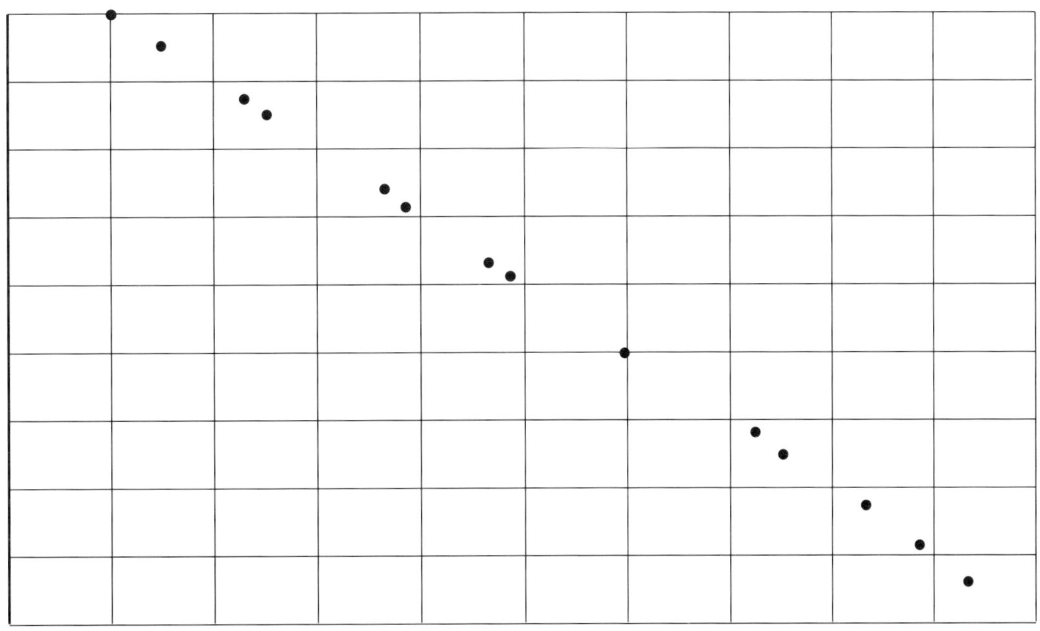

There are, in fact, several alternative formulae for measuring correlation. We will look at one called Spearman's rank order correlation coefficient. The words *rank order* indicate that we do not use the actual data, but rather the positions, or ranks, of the numbers within the set of data.

Example

We will work on the Maths and French marks. We calculate the coefficient as follows:

Stage 1. Calculate the rank in French and Maths for each pupil (for example, pupil A was 10th in French, and 2nd in Maths).

Stage 2. Work out the difference between the two rankings for each pupil

Stage 3. Square the difference for each pupil

Stage 4. Use the following formula for calculating the coefficient

$$r = 1 - \frac{6 \times \sum d^2}{n(n^2 - 1)}$$

where r is the coefficient, $\sum d^2$ is the total of the differences squared and n is the number of pupils.

Pupil	A	B	C	D	E	F	G	H	I	J	
Rank in French	10	6	3	8	1	9	2	5	7	4	
Rank in Maths	2	7	8	3	9	1	10	5	4	6	
Difference in rank (d)	8	1	5	5	8	8	8	0	3	2	
Difference squared (d^2)	64	1	25	25	64	64	64	0	9	4	Total 320

$$n = 10, \text{ so} \qquad r = 1 - \frac{6 \times 320}{10 \times (100 - 1)} \qquad = \frac{64}{33} \qquad = -0.94$$

As this is near -1, we can say that there is strong negative correlation between the French and Maths marks.

4

For each of the following situations, work out the value of Spearman's rank order correlation coefficient and describe in words the correlation.

1.

Pupil	A	B	C	D	E	F	G	H
Rank in Physics	1	2	3	4	5	6	7	8
Rank in Maths	1	2	3	4	5	6	7	8

2.

Pupil	A	B	C	D	E	F	G	H
Rank in English	1	2	3	4	5	6	7	8
Rank in Maths	8	7	6	5	4	3	2	1

3. The runners' height and speed data (First example).

4. The cars' cost and top speed data (Task 1, question 1).

5. The months' rainfall and average temperature data (Task 1, question 2).

6. The patients' drug dosage and length of illness data (Task 1, question 3).

Will you buck the trend?

We saw earlier that sometimes correlation is due to a cause-and-effect process, and at other times there is not such a clear link. However, even when correlation is due to a genuine causal effect, we must remember that correlation is normally never perfect, and that some of the data may not follow the trend. For example, it is sometimes said that there is a positive correlation between unemployment and crime – in areas with higher unemployment, there tends to be more crime.

Do you think that this is true?
If so, why does it happen?

One possible cause is that unemployment leads to people having lots of spare time, with not much to do, and with little spending money, so crime provides both a form of activity and material gain. However, this correlation is not perfect - it does not have a correlation coefficient of +1, and this means that there are many people who do not fit the pattern, just as some tall people are not particularly fast runners.

Even when there is correlation, we still have the moral choice of whether we are going to fit the pattern - go along with the crowd - or whether we are going to do our own thing, based on our thoughts and ideas.

In example 6, a very clever person might choose to work as an Oxfam worker or missionary, in a Third World country, even though the correlation suggests says they could get a high-paid job in more comfortable surroundings.

Should they? What would you do?

5

1. Look back again at the original examples at the start of the Unit. In the cases where you think there is a trend, ask the question:

   "do you have to follow the trend?"

2. Here are some more examples, which may be true or false:
   - The more you are affected by dyslexia, the worse you will do at school.
   - The more you suffer from asthma, the worse you will do at sport.
   - If you come from a one-parent family, you won't succeed in life.

   a) In each case say if you think there is a real trend or not.
   b) If you think there is a trend, can you also think of exceptions to the trend.
   c) Say whether you would want to buck the trend.

Don't overdo it!

6

1. The following data was collected from an agricultural research station, after an experiment to find out how much crop, per hectare, could be produced by adding fertilizer.

Amount of fertiliser (kg)	0	5	10	15	20	25	30	35	40
Yield (tonnes)	0.8	1.3	1.7	2.0	2.2	2.3	2.3	2.2	2.0

a) Plot a scatter diagram of yield against fertilizer.
b) Does it make sense to draw a line of best fit?
c) Is there correlation?
d) How would you account for the pattern?

2. Some transport research students did a large number of one hour long surveys. For each hour they calculated the average speed of cars passing and the average number of cars passing per minute. Some of the results are shown in the table.

Average speed (km/h)	31	52	83	20	69	39	11	90	59
Average no. of cars per minute	39	46	34	34	40	43	24	20	43

a) Plot a scatter diagram of this data.
b) Try to account for any pattern you see.
c) Is there any correlation?

3. In a biological experiment to produce penicillin, the amount produced in one hour was measured, as was the temperature at which the experiment was conducted. The results were:

Temperature (C)	10	15	20	25	30	35	40	45	50	55
Amount (g)	8	14	19	22	24	26	25	20	16	12

a) Plot a scatter diagram of this data.
b) Try to explain any pattern you see.
c) Is there any correlation?

But can you afford it?

UNIT 14

This unit presents the students with a range of financial situations in which they are asked to do relevant calculations. At the same time, they are encouraged to think about their personal responsibility in the areas of borrowing and debt.

Using this unit

The unit is designed primarily for students at the Foundation/ Intermediate Tier of GCSE. The unit involves arithmetic calculations. Although the calculations are not difficult, students may need support to interpret what are sometimes complex contexts. The unit should last for 3–4 hours.

The unit has five main sections in which students consider different personal financial contexts. In each case they learn about the context and do some associated calculations. Some questions encourage them to think about the associated risks and responsibilities in each situation. These can act as a starting point for opening up discussion.

Students need a calculator, protractor and ruler.

Mathematical content

Number (AT2)

- Using a calculator sensibly
- Understanding and calculating with percentages

Spiritual and moral development

The aim of the unit is to encourage students to consider their personal ethical responsibility when making financial decisions, especially those involving debt.

TEACHER'S NOTES

Background

In much of life, it is now the norm to be in debt. We live in a society in which it is now much easier than it used to be to borrow money and purchase goods in advance of payment. There are more and more ways in which people are encouraged to spend money they do not have. The language of debt has changed and people now talk of how "credit" worthy they are. Sadly some people can get into situations of spiralling debt through a combination of credit cards, hire purchase, bank loans, loan sharks etc.

Young people are particularly vulnerable given the great pressures there are on them to spend. This means that there is a need to help students to become aware of the risks and responsibilities associated with their use of money.

Notes on the activities

Hello John, got a new motor?

This first activity focuses on making decisions based on a planned budget. It requires only simple calculations.

Class discussion

The issues raised by this first task could lead to discussion involving:

- the need to plan personal budgets;
- the difficulties that can arise when you have unexpected extra expenditure.

Better drum up some money then

The second activity focuses on different types of hire purchase agreement. It is important that students are clear on the different payment options.

Class discussion

The main issue raised by this task is the pressure to buy now and pay later and the discussion could address:

- the possible merit of saving up for things;
- the circumstances that can lead to difficulties in keeping up with payments (question 6);
- the risks of using a hire purchase agreement (question 7).

There's no place like home

This activity looks at another kind of borrowing which is really another form of debt. To take out a mortgage seems a very reasonable thing to do, but what was a safe investment and a normal thing to do some years ago is now very much more risky. Many people have got into trouble with house prices falling or through redundancy.

It is important that students understand that with a repayment mortgage they are partly paying interest and partly repaying the mortgage. (The model used is slightly simplified in that calculations are based on an annual calculation rather than a monthly calculation.) In question 2, students are asked to copy out and complete the table shown in order to calculate the money owed at the end of Year 2. They are asked to do this twice more in question 3. An optional worksheet with these three tables already prepared is included at the end of these Teacher's Notes.

Question 4 has a potential extension of following through the mortgage payments over 25 years. This would be best tackled using a spreadsheet.

Class discussion

This task addresses the largest debt the students are ever likely to face. The discussion could therefore focus on:

- their own expectations in this area;
- the problem of rising interest rates;
- other risks of having a mortgage such as illness and redundancy.

Paul and his plastic friend

This activity examines the financial costs of using a credit card. As with the mortgage task, the model for calculating interest has been simplified - it is actually charged from the date that each item appears on the account.

Questions 2 and 3 require clear understanding of how the balance and interest is calculated, so some students may require support. A blank statement for question 3 is included at the end of the Teacher's Notes.

Class discussion

This task highlights the large interest charges that can come with credit cards and so the discussion could address:

- advantages of credit cards such as not needing cash, just making a single payment at the end of the month, keeping money in a savings account for longer;
- disadvantages and risks of using credit cards such as the danger of building up debt quickly.

Lend us some dosh, mate

In this final activity the dangers of taking a loan with very high interest is examined.

Question 3 and 5a) are more difficult and some students may need support.

Class discussion

It is good to end the unit by drawing together the students' thoughts on the last task and the unit as a whole. This could include:

- situations that might lead people to take out expensive loans;
- students' reactions to the rate at which interest can build up;
- whether their views on how to save and spend money have been affected by the unit.

Answers

Task 1:

1. £45.
2. £22.50.
3. £42.50.
4. Yes, £2.50 spare.
5. a) and b)

Option 1: Paying in full would require 40 weeks of spare cash, or possibly using luxuries and holiday savings money.

Option 2: Paying the £50 would require 20 weeks of spare cash, or possibly using luxuries and holiday savings money. However, this also leaves John with very little spare cash each week.

Task 2:

1. 9 months.
2. a) £460, 2 months.
   b) £480.
   c) £540.
3. Yes, after 6 months £300 will have been saved. After this each month she saves £50 and pays £90. After 12 months she will be £60 in credit.

Month	1	2	3	4	5	6	7	8	9	10	11	12
Saving	50	50	50	50	50	50	50	50	50	50	50	50
Payment	0	0	0	0	0	0	90	90	90	90	90	90
Balance	50	100	150	200	250	300	260	220	180	140	100	60

4. £45.

Month	1	2	3	4	5	6	7	8	9	10	11	12
Saving	45	45	45	45	45	45	45	45	45	45	45	45
Payment	0	0	0	0	0	0	90	90	90	90	90	90
Balance	45	90	135	180	225	270	225	180	135	90	45	0

5. a) Yes

Month	1	2	3	4	5	6	7	8	9	10	11	12	13	14
Saving	50	50	50	50	50	0	0	50	50	50	50	50	50	50
Payment	0	100	30	30	30	30	30	30	30	30	30	30	30	30
Balance	50	0	20	40	60	30	0	20	40	60	80	100	120	140

b) No

Month	1	2	3	4	5	6	7	8	9	10	11	12
Saving	50	50	50	50	50	0	0	50	50	50	50	50
Payment	40	40	40	40	40	40	40	40	40	40	40	40
Balance	10	20	30	40	50	10	-30	-20	-10	0	10	20

c) No

Month	1	2	3	4	5	6	7	8	9	10	11	12
Saving	50	50	50	50	50	0	0	50	50	50	50	50
Payment	0	0	0	0	0	0	90	90	90	90	90	90
Balance	50	100	150	200	250	250	160	120	80	40	0	-40

d) She would have to delay her purchase by two more months.

6. a) Answers could include sickness, redundancy, other more expensive bills.
   b) This answer should weigh up the relative risks of falling behind on payments and also the value of waiting until money is saved.

Task 3:

1. It is less than 1/25. In the early years more money goes towards interest than repaying what is owed. As time goes by this changes as the interest payments become less and repayment increases.

2. a)

Money owed at the start of year 2		£49,316.16
Interest on amount owed at 8%	8% of £49,316.16	£3,945.29
Total owed	£49316.16 + £3,945.29	£53,261.45
Total payments made by the family	12 x £390.32	£4,683.84
Money owed at end of year 2	£53,261.45 - £4,683.84	£48,577.61

   b) £48,577.61   c) £738.55.
   d) It is more than Year 1 because there was less interest to pay.

3.

Money owed at the start of year 3		£48,577.61
Interest on amount owed at 8%	8% of £48,577.61	£3,886.21
Total owed	£48,577.61 + £3,886.21	£52,463.82
Total payments made by the family	12 x £390.32	£4,683.84
Money owed at end of year 3	£52,463.82 - £4,683.84	£47,779.98

Money owed at the start of Year 4		£47,779.98
Interest on amount owed at 8%	8% of £47,779.98	£3,822.40
Total owed	£47,779.98 + £3,822./40	£51,602.38
Total payments made by the family	12 x £390.32	£4,683.84
Money owed at end of Year 4	£51,602.38 - £4,683.84	£46,918.54

   a) £47,779.98.   b) £46,918.54.
   c) £797.63.   d) £861.44.

4. The amount owed at the end of each year over the 25 years is as follows:
   yr1-£49316.16; yr2-£48577.61; yr3-£47779.98; yr4-£46918.54; yr5-£45988.18; yr6-£44983.40; yr7-£43898.23; yr8-£42726.25; yr9-£41460.51; yr10-£40093.51; yr11-£38617.15; yr12-£37022.68; yr13-£35300.66; yr14-£33440.87; yr15-£31432.20; yr16-£29263.04; yr17-£26920.25; yr18-£24390.03; yr19-£21657.39; yr20-£18706.14; yr21-£15518.79; yr22-£12076.45; yr23-£8358.73; yr24-£4343.59; yr25-£7.23.
   a) If the interest rate is lowered then the length of time for the mortgage decreases or (more usually) the monthly payment is reduced.
   b) If the interest is raised then the length of time is extended or (more usually) the monthly payment is increased.

5. The risks include not being able to keep up the payments:
   - if interest rates increase significantly;
   - if income decreases through sickness, redundancy or change of job;
   - if expenditure increases significantly through children, household goods.

Task 4:

1. a) £122.99. b) £6.15.
2. a) £110.45. b) £5.52.

3.

Date	Reference	Description	Amount
		Balance from previous statement Interest of 2% on £110.45	£110.45 £2.21
3 April		Amount owed Payment received	£112.66 £5.52
		New balance	£107.14
		Minimum payment due by 4 May	£5.36

4. a) Advantages: No need to carry cash, payment put off until end of month.
   b) Disadvantages: High interest rates, temptation to buy more than you can afford.

Task 5:

1. £5.
2. £30.
3. a) £6.
   b) £36.
4. a) £43.20.
   b) 4 weeks, £51.84 owed.
5. b) 8 weeks, £107.50 owed.
   c) 21 weeks, £1150.13 owed.
6. a) Answers might include wanting to pay off other debts or not being able to get credit on something you really want to buy.
   b) Answers might include the shock of how quickly the debt has increased.

Task 3:

Question 2

Year 2

Money owed at the start of year 2		£49,316.16
Interest on amount owed at 8%	8% of £49,316.16	
Total owed	£49,316.16 +	
Total payments made by the family	12 x £390.32	£4,683.84
Money owed at end of year 2	- £4,683.84	

Question 3

Year 3

Money owed at the start of year 3		
Interest on amount owed at 8%	8% of	
Total owed		
Total payments made by the family	12 x £390.32	
Money owed at end of year 3		

Year 4

Money owed at the start of year 4		
Interest on amount owed at 8%		
Total owed		
Total payments made by the family		
Money owed at end of year 4		

Task 4:

Question 3

Date	Reference	Description	Amount
		Balance from previous statement Interest of 2% on	
30 Mar		Amount owed Payment received	
		New balance	
		Minimum payment due by 3 May	

But can you afford it?

UNIT 14

There are many occasions when you have to make difficult decisions about how to use your money. This unit looks at five sorts of situations which you might face at some time. In each case you will be considering "But can I afford it?"

"Hello John, got a new motor?"

When making decisions about using your money, it is a good idea to know what your income and expenditure is likely to be. In this first task, you have to advise John on how to organise his weekly budget.

1

John earns £250 per week.
His outgoings (what he spends his money on) are, on average, as follows:

Accommodation	£60
Bills (telephone, gas, electricity)	£40
Council tax	£10
Food	£35
Essentials (clothes, etc.)	£15
Luxuries (outings, drinks etc.)	£15
Saving for holidays	£10
Transport to get to work by bus	£20

1. How much money does John have left each week?

2. John does some research into buying a car. He estimates that the running costs per week would be as follows:

Insurance	£5.00
Tax	£2.50
Petrol	£10.00
6 monthly service	£5.00

   How much will it cost him to run his car per week on the basis of these figures?

3. If he decides to buy the car, how much money will he now have left each week? (Remember, he no longer needs to spend any money on public transport.)

4. In order to do this he needs to buy the car. He has found one that he can buy, but will have to pay instalments on the purchase of the car of £40 per week. Can he afford this?

1

Task 1 continued

5. Suppose now that he has an accident and the bill for repairs will cost £100. He has a choice:

Option 1: He can pay the full £100 himself.
Option 2: He can pay the first £50 himself but could claim the other £50 from the insurance company. If he does this then his insurance payments will go up to £7.00 per week.

a) What should he do? Write down in detail which choice you think he should make and why.
b) Give details of any adjustments you would suggest he makes to his weekly budget.

Do you know how much you spend on different things each week?

"Better drum up some money, then"

These days, not only do you have to consider whether you are going to buy something, but also how you are going to pay for it. In this second task, you have to help Clare decide how to pay for her drums.

2

Clare's band are starting to get gigs and she wants to get her own drum kit. She has seen one in a music shop for £450.

1. Clare thinks she can save about £50 per month. How many months would she need to save in order to have enough money to buy the kit?

2. Clare finds out that the shop offers different payment options. In each case she could have the kit more quickly than if she saved up for the whole amount.

Option A: Pay a deposit of £100 and then pay £30 per month for 12 months with the first instalment one month after the deposit.
Option B: Pay no deposit, take the kit immediately and pay £40 per month for 12 months with the first instalment one month after taking the kit.
Option C: Pay no deposit, take the kit immediately and pay £90 per month for 6 months with the first instalment six months after taking the kit.

a) How much does Option A cost in total? How long would she have to wait before she could afford this option?
b) How much does Option B cost in total?
c) How much does Option C cost in total?

2

Task 2 continued

3. Will Clare be able to keep up the payments on option C?

4. What is the minimum that Clare would have to save each month if she were to pay by Option C?

5. Imagine Clare has a crisis in months 6 and 7 and does not save anything in either month.
   a) Would she be able to keep up the payments for Option A?
   b) Would she be able to keep up the payments for Option B?
   c) Would she be able to keep up the payments for Option C?
   d) What effect would the crisis have on the saving method of question 1?

6. a) What kind of circumstances might occur to prevent Clare saving for two months?
   b) Explain which of the four methods of payment you would advise her to use and why.

7. The three options offered by the shop involve a risk because Clare is promising to pay money which she expects to have but cannot be certain of having.
   a) What are the chances of not having it?
   b) What risks would you be prepared to take if you were in her place?

Do you prefer to buy now and pay later or save up and then buy?

"There's no place like home"

One of the biggest decisions you may ever make is whether to buy a house. Almost everyone does this by taking out a mortgage with a building society or bank. One type of mortgage is known as a Repayment Mortgage. This allows you to pay back the money you owe over a long period of time by paying a fixed amount each month. Each year the money you give the building society goes partly towards the interest on what you owe and partly towards repaying some of the mortgage. In this next task you will help the Walker family with their mortgage decisions.

3

Mr and Mrs Walker have seen a house for £50,000 that they would like to buy. They will need a 100% mortgage – this means that they would borrow all of the £50,000. They also decide that they want a 25-year mortgage – this means they would pay the money back over 25 years. At the time of the purchase the interest rate is 8% p.a. and the building society calculates that this requires a monthly payment of £390.32. The table shows how the first year would work out.

Money owed at the start of year 1		£50,000.00
Interest on amount owed at 8%	8% of 50000	£4,000.00
Total owed	£50,000 + £4,000	£54,000
Total payments made by the family	12 x £390.32	£4,683.84
Money owed at end of year 1	£54,000.00 – £4,683.84	£49,316.16

Amount of mortgage repaid = £50,000 - £49,316.16 = £683.84

3

Task 3 continued

1. The amount of mortgage paid back is £683.84. Is this more or less than 1/25 of the £50,000 that the Walkers owe the building society?. Explain why, in spite of this, the debt would be paid off in 25 years.
2. a) Now copy the table for year 2.

Money owed at the start of year 2		£49,316.16
Interest on amount owed at 8%	8% of £49,316.16	
Total owed		
Total payments made by the family	12 x £390.32	
Money owed at end of year 2		

   b) By filling in the gaps, work out how much is owed at the end of year 2.
   c) Work out the amount of mortgage repaid during year 2.
   d) What do you notice about the amount of mortgage repaid that year? How do you explain it?
3. Now do the calculations for years 3 and 4 by constructing a table for each year.
   a) How much is owed at the end of year 3?
   b) How much is owed at the end of year 4?
   c) How much of the mortgage was repaid in year 3?
   d) How much of the mortgage was repaid in year 4?
4. The sum of £390.32 per month is calculated so that the total debt is paid off in 25 years, assuming the interest rate does not change. (You could check to see if it really does work out over the 25 years!)
   a) What do you think happens if the interest rate is lowered?
   b) What do you think happens if it is raised?
5. The Walker family takes on this mortgage because they feel that they can afford to pay the £390.32 per month. What are the possible risks of doing this?

What hopes do you have for a home in the future?
Do you expect to buy a house one day?

"Paul and his plastic friend"

One way many people pay for goods is with a credit card. All you have to do in the shop is sign a receipt, which is then sent to the central office of the credit card company. All transactions are added up and at the end of the month you receive a statement. You must then decide how much to pay. (Some shops also have their own store cards which operate in a similar way to credit cards.) In this next task you will help Paul with his credit card decisions.

4

1. Paul's statement for February has only three items.

Date	Reference	Description	Amount
16Feb.	8JZYRE9	Longmoor Rd Service St.	24.99
19Feb	B2ERTF7	Helen Hotel, Matlock	54.40
20Feb	3WDBJI6	British Rail, Manchester	43.60
		Total	
		Minimum payment to arrive by 4 Mar	

a) What is the total he owes the credit card company?
b) Work out 5% of the total.
c) Paul must pay a minimum payment of either £5 or 5% of the bill, whichever is the larger. How much will Paul have to pay?

2. If Paul pays his statement in full by the date stated he is not charged any interest. However, if the total amount is not paid off, interest of 2% is added to the total. This appears on the following month's statement. Paul's March statement shows that he decided only to pay £15 by the due date and also that he did not use his card in March.

Date	Reference	Description	Amount
		Balance from previous statement Interest of 2% on 122.99	122.99 2.46
4Mar		Amount owed Payment received	125.45 15.00
		New balance	
		Minimum payment due by 3 Apr	

a) What is the total that Paul now owes the credit card company?
b) What is his minimum payment?

3. If Paul just pays the minimum in March and does not use his credit card in April, what will his April statement look like?

4. The rate of interest (2% per month), if worked out for the whole year, would be very much higher than the borrowing rate from the bank.
a) What are the advantages of credit cards?
b) What are the disadvantages or risks of using a credit card?

5. What advice would you give Paul when he comes to pay his April statement?

Have you ever been in debt to someone?

"Lend us some dosh, mate"

Sometimes people get into situations where they are desperate for money. It is at times like this that they may go to a money lender. Some money lenders charge very high interest rates and it is easy for the debt to build up. In this task you will see the difficulty that Andy can get into quite quickly.

5

Andy needs £25 and decides to borrow from a money lender. The conditions are:

- everything must be repaid within six months;
- he can pay back what he owes at any time within that period;
- interest will be added to the total he owes on a weekly basis;
- interest will first be charged one week after he borrows the money;
- the interest is charged at 20% per week on anything that is owed.

1. What is 20% of £25?

2. How much does he owe at the end of the first week if he can not pay anything back, including the interest?

3. In later weeks, if he has not paid anything back, he is also charged 20% interest on the interest he owes.
   a) How much interest is charged in week 2?
   b) How much does he owe at the end of week 2?

4. Andy is unable to pay anything back in the next few weeks as well.
   a) How much does he owe at the end of week 3?
   b) Find how many weeks elapse before the amount owed is doubled (£50).

5. A quick way to calculate how much is owed at the end of each week is to multiply the previous week's debt by 1.2.
   a) Explain why this works.
   b) Find how many weeks elapse before the sum owed is £100.
   c) Find how many weeks elapse before the sum owed is £1000.

6. a) Write down some situations in which you might be tempted to borrow £25 at a weekly interest rate of 20%.
   b) How would you feel if you had borrowed £25 without being able to pay it back and found yourself owing £1000.

Imagine you lent a friend some money to buy lunch and he said he would pay you back the next day.

How would you feel if he did not pay you back?

Would you borrow money when there is a possibility that you cannot pay it back?

Mr Kepler's shapes

UNIT 15

In this unit, the students engage in a range of activities with shape whilst considering how geometry can contribute to our appreciation of the universe. They also learn about the mathematician Kepler and his work.

Mathematical content

Shape and Space (AT3)

- Describing and constructing symmetrical shapes
- Nets and polyhedra
- Constructing curves and loci

Using this unit

The unit is intended to be accessible to students at all tiers of GCSE.

The unit is expected to take about 3 hours. There are three sections in the unit. Each section could be done in a long lesson, with scope for homework as well. The sections do not all have to be done at the same time but, if they are done at different times, reference will need to be made to earlier work. Each one relates to a different aspect of Kepler's work and contain descriptions of his work and some quotations from his writings. There are core and extension activities for different elements of shape and space work. It is recommended that each section begins with a whole class discussion/thinking activity. Each section offers opportunity for student reflection.

Spiritual and moral development

The aim of the unit is to promote a sense of wonder for the students about the Universe in which they live. It also aims to develop their awareness of how religious belief can both motivate and stimulate the work of mathematicians and scientists.

There are practical elements to the work so students will need access to drawing equipment and suitable paper/card for the polyhedra work. Templates for squares, equilateral triangles and regular pentagons would be useful. Already constructed regular solids would also be helpful.

TEACHER'S NOTES

Background

Kepler is best known for his work on planetary motion. Less often mentioned is the passion he had to make known the glory of God's works in creation. His faith in God convinced him that there must be a harmony in the universe. This in turn convinced him of the mathematical design of the Universe and that explanations of the world needed a thorough grounding in geometry. Nevertheless, he was always keen to check his theories against observations and he also sought plausible physical causes.

In *The Six-Cornered Snowflake*, Kepler sought to explain the hexagonal symmetry through geometry. He saw a fundamental connection between the formation of a snowflake in the atmosphere, the constructions of a honeycomb by a family of bees and the growth of a pomegranate. According to his theory, the regular, symmetrical patterns that arise in each case can be described and explained in terms of "space-filling geometric figures".

In both *The Mystery of the Cosmos* and *The New Astronomy*, he used his knowledge of Greek geometry as sources of ideas for new theories. Euclid's *Elements* and Appolonius' *Conics* were highly regarded textbooks in Kepler's day and these would have introduced him to the regular (Platonic) solids and to the ellipse as a conic section, respectively.

Additional sources

Morris Kline, *Mathematics in Western Culture* (Penguin, 1990)
Ian Stewart and Martin Golubitsky, *Fearful Symmetry – Is God a Geometer?* (Penguin 1992)
John Fauvel and Jeremy Gray (eds), *The History of Mathematics – A Reader* (Open University, 1987)
Keith Devlin, *Mathematics – The Science of Patterns* (Scientific American Library, 1994)
Istvan Hargittai and Magdolna Hargittai, *Symmetry – A Unifying Concept* (Shelter Publications, 1994)

Polydron, Clixi or ATM Mats all offer alternative ways of exploring nets and polyhedra.

Notes on the activities

In each of the three sections, there is a quotation from Kepler's writing followed by some questions which are there to encourage the students to reflect. In order for this to be effective:

- students must be given time to focus upon the questions on their own;
- students must be encouraged to make a response, either through writing or contributing to class discussion;
- students' views must be respected by the class;
- the end of lessons could be given over to this kind of reflective period.

The Six-cornered Snowflake

Start this section by putting up an acetate of the snowflakes (if OHP is not available, then worksheets could be copied). Give them time to appreciate the images.

Ask students to say what they notice about the snowflakes. Get them to describe any patterns, shapes or symmetry that they see. As necessary, make sure they are clear that all snowflakes have hexagonal symmetry. Following this the snowflake sheet can be issued. You may wish to demonstrate the snowflake construction to the whole class.
A possible extension task not suggested on the sheet is to explore creating snowflake images using LOGO.

The Mystery of the Cosmos

Start this section by asking students to try to imagine solid shapes for which all the faces are identical. Ask individual students to describe or draw their solids for the rest of the class. (This could then extend into a practical investigation if time were available.) Alternatively, the sheet could be issued and the five solids discussed.

You will need to decide how you want the students to produce the nets in question 2. This will depend on available resources and the extent to which you wish drawing skills to be developed. Question 4 is really an extension task and requires some quite high level reasoning.

The New Astronomy

Start this section by asking students to imagine what shapes you get if you slice a cylinder in different ways. It will help if you have some way of demonstrating the slicing process. Make sure that they see that the cross-section can be either a circle or an ellipse. (A possible extension to this is to use a double cone and include also the parabola and the hyperbola.)

Some students may need a demonstration of some of the ellipse construction methods. The methods in question 1 and 2 can be extended by exploring what happens when you have the point P in different places. Do you still get an ellipse? Is it the same?

Answers

Task 1:

1. a) rotational symmetry of order 3; rotational and reflection symmetry of order 6; rotational and reflection symmetry of order 4; rotational and reflection symmetry of order 6.
   b) Shape 2 and Shape 4 could be snowflakes because of their rotational and reflection symmetry of order 6.

4. a) Use the same method as before but start with 6, 8, 10 and 16 sectors respectively.

Task 2

1.

Name	Number of faces	Number of edges	Number of vertices
Tetrahedron	4	6	4
Cube	6	12	8
Octahedron	8	12	6
Dodecahedron	12	30	20
Icosahedron	20	30	12

3. a) $F + V = E + 2$.

4. Students can be encouraged to explore the different ways of arranging regular shapes in a net so that at least three edges join to make a vertex. Once a hexagon or above is considered the interior angles become too large. For pentagons and squares the maximum possible number of edges at a vertex is 3 (dodecagon and cube). For triangles 3, 4 and 5 edges can meet at a vertex (tetrahedron, octahedron, icosahedron) but not 6. This is therefore an exhaustive list of the possible regular solids.

TEACHER'S NOTES

Mr Kepler's shapes

UNIT 15

In this unit, you will be doing a variety of shape activities, but you will also be learning about an important mathematician, Johannes Kepler, and what he understood about the Universe.

The six-cornered snowflake

Johannes Kepler lived from 1571 to 1630 in different places in Germany, Austria and the Czech Republic. He was a mathematician, astronomer and scientist. He went to University in Tubingen when he was 16. It was said of him there that he had "such a superior and magnificent mind that something special may be expected of him".

In about 1600, Johannes Kepler wrote a remarkable essay called the *Six-Cornered Snowflake*. It was written as a New Year's present to Johann Matthaus Wacker von Wackenfels, the man who paid his salary. Kepler knew that all snowflakes had rotational symmetry and reflection symmetry both of order 6. He wondered why this was so. He thought very hard about it and, using his knowledge of shape, concluded that it was something to do with packing objects as closely together as possible.

1

1. Look at the diagrams alongside.
   a) Describe the symmetry of each of the shapes
   b) Which of them could be diagrams of snowflakes?
   Explain how you know.

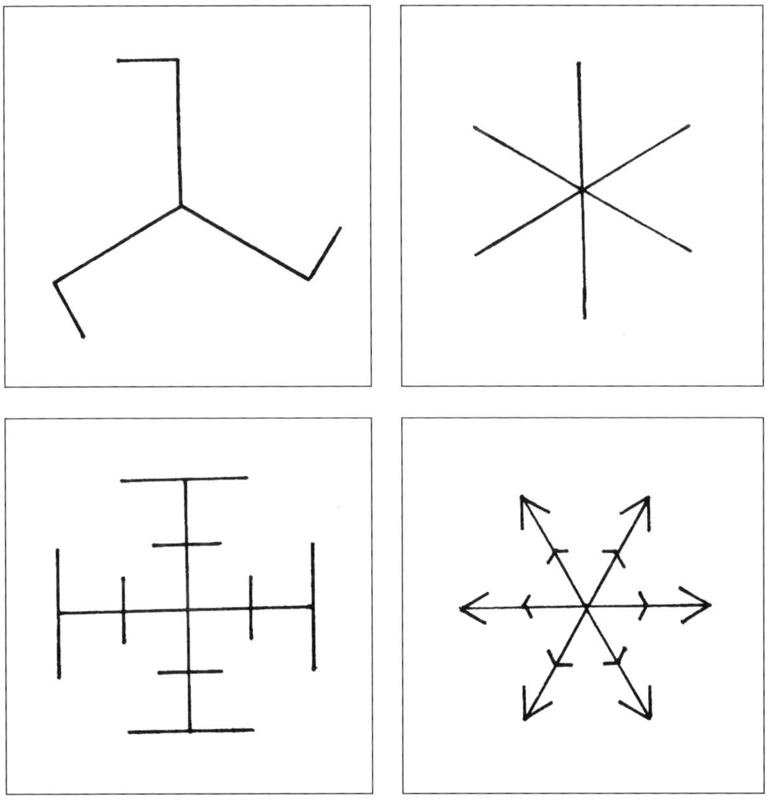

1

Task 1 continued

2. Follow the stages described below in order to produce a snowflake image.

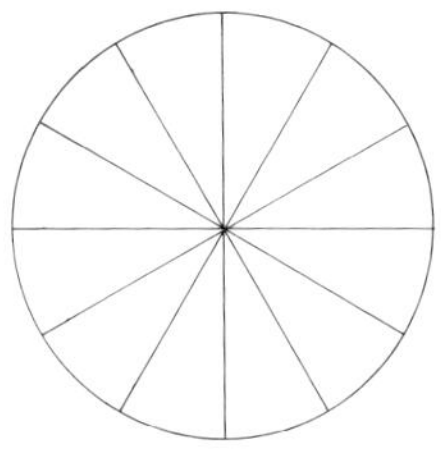

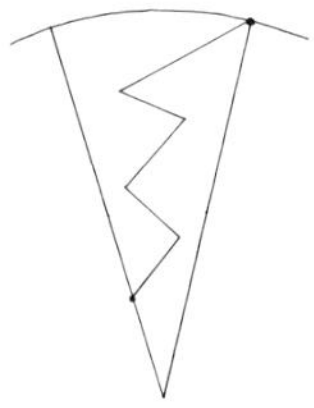

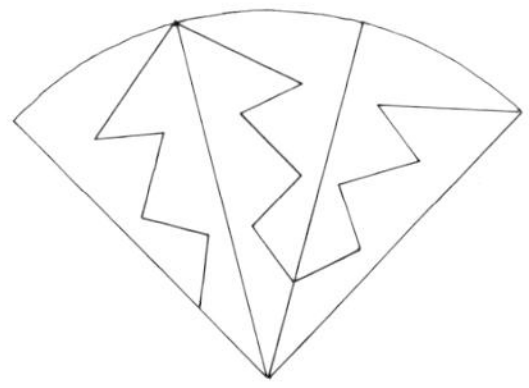

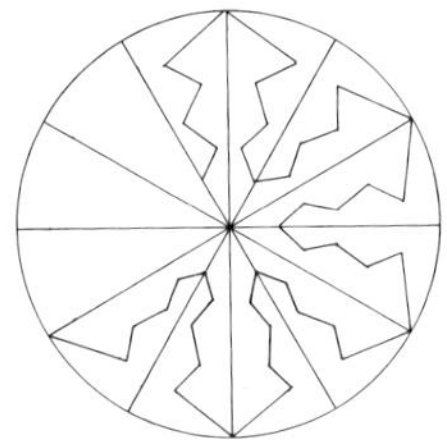

Stage 1:
On a piece of plain A4 paper, draw a circle of radius 8 cm and divide it into 12 equal sectors

Stage 2:
Choose two adjacent sector lines. Mark a point on one at the circumference and mark a point on the other at about 2 cm from the centre. Then join the two points with a line design like the one shown.

Stage 3:
Draw the reflection of the pattern in one of the sector lines. Then reflect this image in the next sector line.

Stage 4:
Continue this reflection process around the circle until the snowflake is produced. Then cut out the final shape.

3. You can produce more complex snowflakes by changing your line design. Try the method again, but this time use a more complicated line design.

4. Snowflakes have rotational symmetry of order 6.
   a) How would you adapt the method in question 2 to produce shapes with rotational symmetry of order 3, 4, 5 or 8?
   b) Use these adapted methods to produce some shapes with different orders of rotational symmetry.

I thank thee O Lord our Creator, that thou hast permitted me to look at the beauty in thy work of creation. I exalt thee in the works of thy hands.

Kepler in *Harmony of the World*

Kepler was fascinated enough by snowflakes to write an essay.

- How do you react to the beauty and complexity of snowflakes?
- Have you ever been amazed by the beauty of other things in the natural world?
- Do you ever take time to stop and look more closely at the natural world you see around you?
- Do you ever take time to wonder why things are like they are?

The mystery of the cosmos

In 1594, Kepler was encouraged to leave university and to take up the post of astronomy teacher and professor of mathematics and morals in Ganz, South Austria. It was about a year later when he had an amazing idea one Summer afternoon which led him to write and publish his book *The Mystery of the Cosmos* or *The Cosmographic Secret.*

At that time, there were only six known planets: Mercury; Venus; Earth; Mars; Jupiter and Saturn. Kepler wanted to explain why there were exactly six planets and why they were at particular distances from the Sun. He experimented with lots of different ideas until he arrived at a model that fitted with there being only 5 regular solids. In this model, the orbits of the planets were on the surface of spheres. Each solid was carefully chosen to work out accurately the size and position of the next sphere. Each time the solid nested perfectly inside the next sphere and the sphere perfectly inside the next solid.

Kepler's diagram shows his idea: the outer sphere (on which Saturn moves) contains a cube, inside which is a sphere for the orbit of Jupiter. In that sphere was a tetrahedron and the sphere inside that was for Mars' orbit. Next came the dodecahedron with a sphere inside for the Earth's orbit, followed by the icosahedron with the Venus sphere after that. Finally came the octahedron with the Mercury sphere inside this again. Had he solved the mystery of the Cosmos? Sadly, Kepler's very imaginative idea was wrong. The spheres were not quite right and we of course now know that there are at least nine planets.

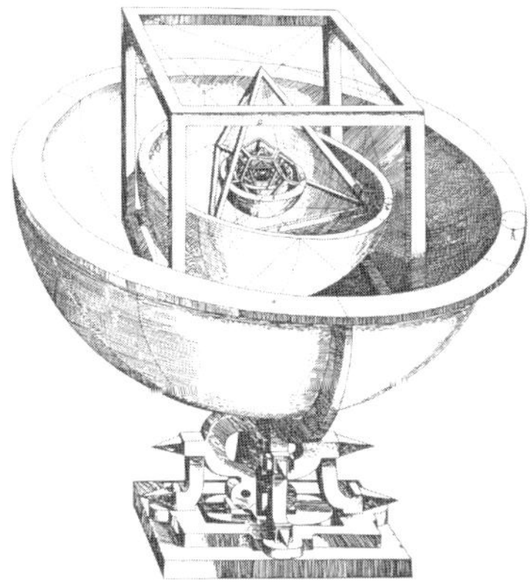

Kepler's planetary model

2

1. For each of the regular solids, complete the table.

Name	Number of faces	Number of edges	Number of vertices
Tetrahedron			
Cube			
Octahedron			
Dodecahedron			
Icosahedron			

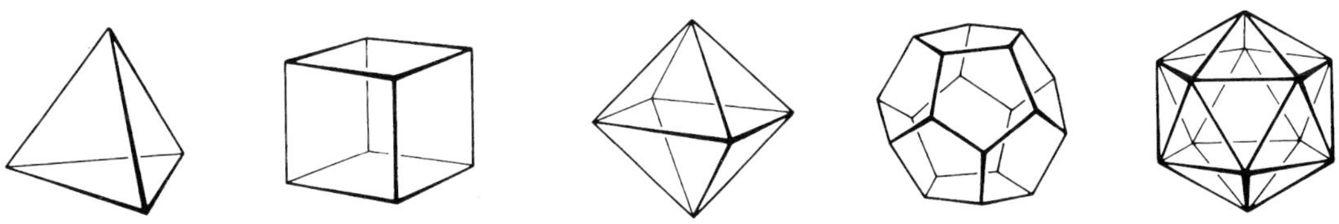

Regular solids

2

Task 2 continued

2. For each of the solids construct a net. Try folding the net to produce the solid. You may find it helpful to use a template to draw the net. Alternatively, your teacher may have equipment you can use for constructing solids.

3. There is a connection between the number of faces, edges and vertices of the regular solids.
   a) Try to work out the connection and write it as a formula. It is normally called Euler's formula.
   b) Investigate to see if the formula works for other solids as well.

4. Can you explain why there are no more than five regular solids?

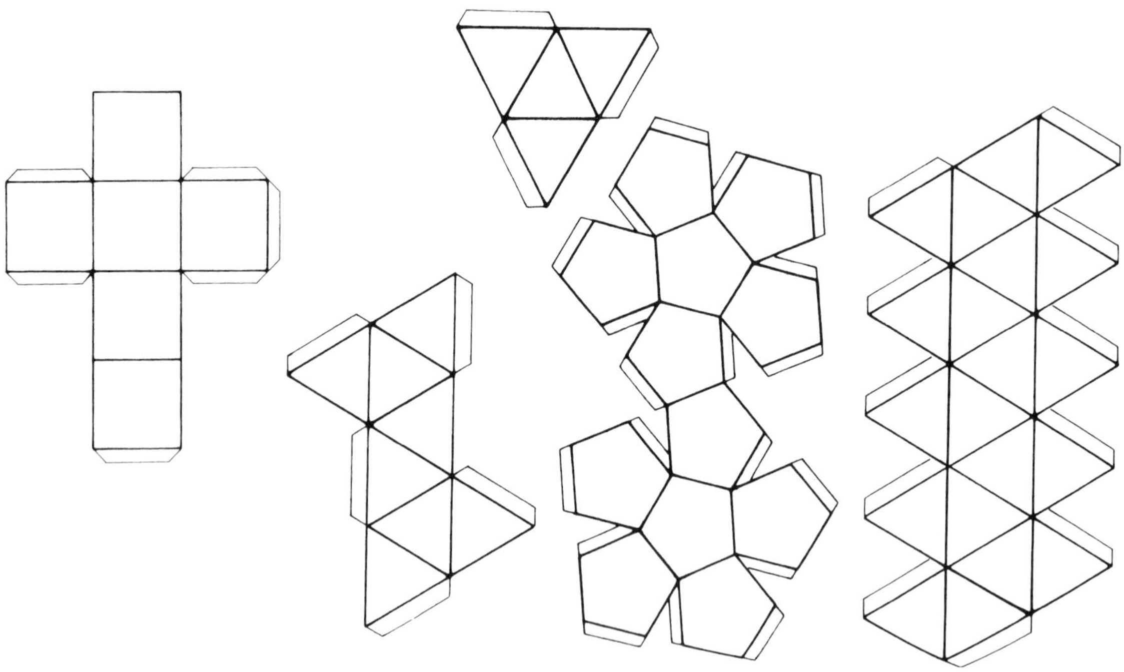

Happy the man who devotes himself to the study of the heavens;
he learns to set less value on what the world admires most;
the works of God are for him above all else, and their study will furnish him
with the purest of enjoyments.
Kepler in the preface of *The Mystery of the Cosmos*

Kepler's response to the patterns he found in the heavens was to praise God.

- Have you ever spent time just gazing at the night sky?
- How do you respond to the amazing Universe in which we live?

The new astronomy

Although Kepler's idea in the *Mystery of the Cosmos* was not accepted, it did bring him into contact with Tyco Brahe, the leading astronomer of the day. By 1600, Kepler was working as an assistant to Brahe in Prague. Kepler's task was to observe the orbit of Mars. Brahe died in 1601 and Kepler took over as imperial mathematician to Emperor Rudolf II. He continued to examine the orbit of the planet Mars and in 1609 he published a book called *The New Astronomy*.

Kepler thought that there was great harmony in the world and so expected any explanations of the world to require geometry. At the time, people believed that the orbits of the planets had to be related to circles because circles were perfect shapes. However, this meant that they needed a very complicated system of circles with centres that moved in circles and so on. Kepler had the inspired idea to give up on the circle and consider the ellipse instead. This was a shape mathematicians had known about for almost 2000 years. By choosing the ellipse for an orbit, everything became very simple and Kepler was convinced that he had found a better theory.

3

1. Follow the stages below to construct an ellipse.

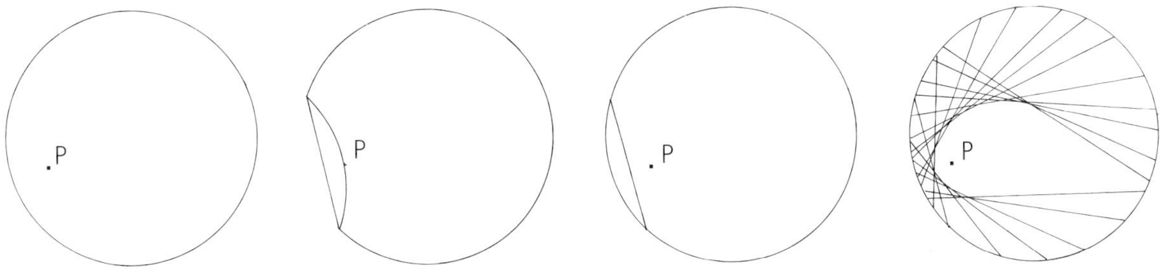

Stage 1:
Cut out a circle of radius 8 cm and mark a point P quite close to the edge.

Stage 2:
Fold the circle over so that the circumference just touches the point.

Stage 3:
Unfold the circle and go over the crease in pencil.

Stage 4:
Continue folding and drawing until the ellipse becomes clear.

3

Task 3 continued

2. Follow the stages for this alternative method for constructing an ellipse.

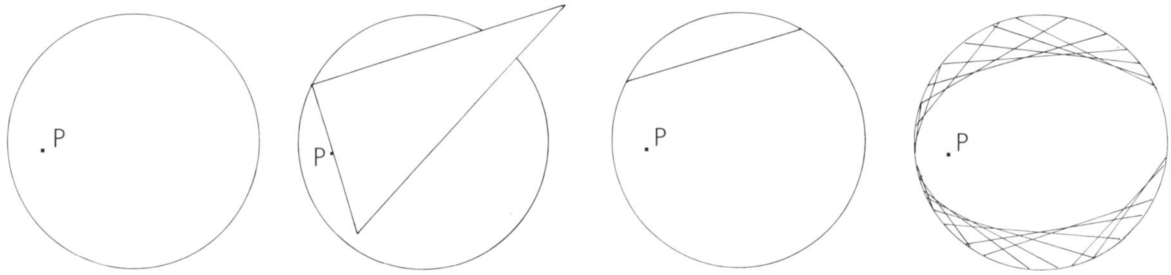

Stage 1:
Draw a circle of radius 4 cm and mark a point P near the edge.

Stage 2:
Place a set square so that one edge touches P and the right angle is on the circumference of the circle.

Stage 3:
Draw the chord of the circle made by the other side.

Stage 4:
Repeat stages 2 and 3 for different set square positions until the ellipse becomes clear

3. Follow the stages for a final method for constructing an ellipse.

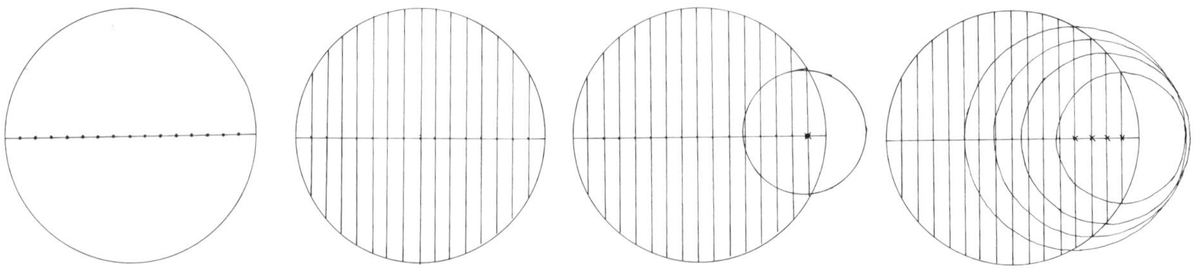

Stage 1:
Draw a circle of radius 4 cm and mark off points every 5mm along a diameter.

Stage 2:
At each of the marked points draw chords perpendicular to the diameter.

Stage 3:
Choose one of the lines and treat it as a diameter of a circle. Draw that circle.

Stage 4:
Repeat the process for all of the perpendicular lines.

> The wisdom of the Lord is infinite, so also are His glory and His power ...
> To Him be praise, honour and glory throughout eternity.
> Kepler in *Harmony of the World*

Kepler believed that as he studied the world with its amazing harmony he would also discover more about God.

- Do you have a desire to know more about the world?
- If you do, explain what and why. If you do not, also try to explain why.
- What is it that motivates you to study?

The inside story

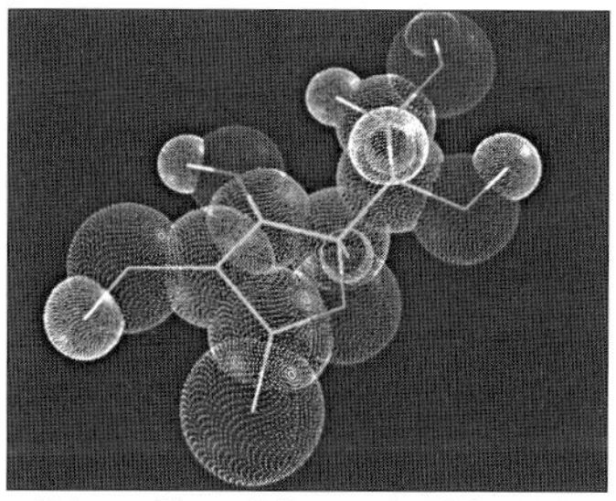
Science Photo Library: A. PASIEKA

UNIT 16

In this unit, molecular structure provides a context within which students work on standard form for numbers less than one. They also explore current scientific models for the development of the Universe and consider scientists' views about whether human life is a cosmic accident or not.

Mathematical content

Number (AT2)
- Positive and negative powers of ten
- Standard form for all numbers
- Manipulation of numbers in standard form

Algebra (AT2)
- Substitution in formulae

Using this unit

The unit is intended for students at the Intermediate/Higher Tier of GCSE. Students are expected to be familiar with the concept of standard form for numbers greater than ten (this is covered in the unit *The Designer Universe?*). There is only a brief note on standard form for numbers less than one in the text, so the students will need to have been taught this before they attempt the unit. The unit is expected to take about 1½ to 2 hours.

It begins by examining the spiritual issue at the heart of the unit - are human beings important in our vast and complex Universe? This is returned to in the concluding sections by considering quotations from eminent scientists. The rest of the unit uses different contexts in which students practise using standard form for numbers less than one. The difficulty of the tasks increases throughout the unit.

Spiritual and moral development

The unit aims to promote a sense of wonder about the Universe. Students are also encouraged to reflect on the origins of the Universe and their place within it.

Students will need a calculator for tasks 3 and 4 (they will need to be able to enter numbers in standard form and interpret answers shown in standard form).

TEACHER'S NOTES

Background

Many people assume that modern scientific theories about the development of the Universe and life on Earth contradict Christian beliefs about creation and the existence of a loving God. This unit seeks to investigate this view by inviting students to consider the conditions required before life could develop. For some scientists, the need for these very precise conditions can suggest the activity of a purposeful designer. This coincides with views found in religious writing such as the Psalmist quoted at the start of the unit.

In *The Designer Universe?* students were asked to consider the special conditions which exist on Earth which make it suitable for the development of life. This unit continues this theme. Life on Earth could not have developed unless conditions in the early Universe were very precisely controlled. A few elementary scientific ideas are introduced in the unit but many of the ideas within this field are beyond the scope of this unit.

Interested teachers and students can explore the ideas in this unit further by reading either of the first two books in 'Additional Sources'. Both are available in paperback and easy to read. The writers of the unit are aware that some Christians may not accept current theories about the development of the Universe and life on Earth. Such theories are only scientific models, but they are nonetheless widely accepted amongst eminent scientists, many of whom are Christians.

Additional sources

Books:

John Polkinghorne, *Quarks, Chaos and Christianity* (Triangle 1994)
John Houghton, *The Search for God – Can Science Help?* (Lion 1995)
Michael Poole, *A Guide to Science and Belief* (Lion 1994)
P. C. W. Davies, *The Accidental Universe* (Cambridge University Press 1982)
A. Watts, *The World of the Atom* (Aladdin Books Ltd. 1989)
Glen and Susan Toole, *Understanding Biology for Advanced Level* (Stanley Thornes 1995)
Littlefield and Thorley, *Atomic and Nuclear Physics* (D. van Nostrand Co. Ltd. 1963)
Further Science from the 'Science at Work' series (Longman 1993)

Posters:

The London Planetarium, Marylebone Road, London, NW1. (0171-935-6861)

TEACHER'S NOTES

Notes on the Activities

Where do we fit in

In this first section, the spiritual content of the unit is introduced. A wall display of pictures of stars, galaxies and planets could incorporate some of the students' answers to question 4 in task 1. The London Planetarium has some excellent posters.

Class discussion

The students' responses to task 1 can provide the basis for a whole class discussion. In particular the following can be addressed:

- their thoughts on the size and age of the Universe;
- their understanding of the Psalmist's writing;
- their views on their own place within the universe.

How big is "small"?

In this section, students are asked to interpret numbers in standard form and to compare them.

Splitting the atom

In this section, students work on the structure of the atom. Task 3, question 3 requires the students to manipulate numbers in standard form. A calculator would be useful.

Exploding stars

The section begins with examining the importance of carbon. Students should have their attention drawn to the Polkinghorne quotation. A calculator is needed from question 2 in task 4 onwards.

So what is the inside story?

In the final section, the significance of the ideas explored in the previous sections is examined. Students could be asked to write their response to the final question as a preparation for a class discussion.

Class discussion

The unit would be best finished by discussing together the students' thoughts on the following:

- the origins of the Universe: accident/chance versus design;
- the impact on our lives of our views about the origins of the Universe.

Answers

Task 2:

1. a) 0.01; b) 0.0001; c) 0.000000001; d) 0.000001; e) 0.001.
2. cell 1×10^{-2}; bacteria 1×10^{-3}; virus 1×10^{-4}; molecule 1×10^{-6}; atom $\times 10^{-9}$.
3. cell.
4. a) false; b) true; c) true; d) false.

Task 3:

1. a) proton and neutron; b) electron, proton, neutron; c) 2000 (accept 1000).
2. a) 10^3 (or 1000);
   b) proton 1.672×10^{-24}g, neutron 1.675×10^{-24}g, electron 9.11×10^{-28}g.
3. a) 2.6776×10^{-26} kg; b) 2.26×10^{-28} kg.

Task 4:

1. a) 1×10^{-2} seconds; b) 2×10^{2} seconds; c) 1,000,000,000 °K; d) 1×10^{6} years; e) 1×10^{7} years; f) 1×10^{10} years.
2. 2×10^{24} in a gram; 2×10^{27} in a kg.
3. 2×10^{19} in a second; 2×10^{16} in a millisecond.
4. 10^6 or 1 million.
5. a) $M_{hydrogen} = 1.66 \times 10^{-27}$ kg;
   $M_{carbon} = 1.992 \times 10^{-26}$ kg;
   $M_{oxygen} = 2.656 \times 10^{-26}$ kg.
   b) $R_{hydrogen} = 1.4 \times 10^{-15}$ m;
   $R_{carbon} = 3.205 \times 10^{-15}$ m (to 4 significant figures);
   $R_{oxygen} = 3.528 \times 10^{-15}$ m (to 4 significant figures).

The inside story

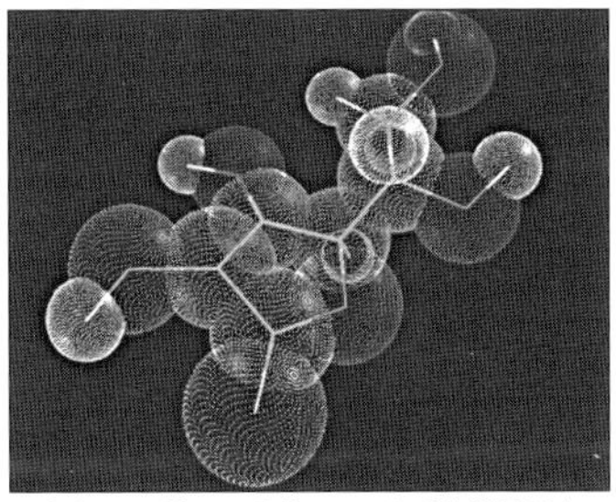

Science Photo Library: A. PASIEKA

UNIT 16

Where do we fit in?

Some scientists believe that our huge and wonderful Universe has been designed just so people like you and me could exist! If you have studied the unit, *The Designer Universe?*, you will have learnt about the way our Earth is ideally suited to the development of life.

In this unit we will think about the development of our Universe and consider the idea that its whole history has been necessary for the creation of living beings like ourselves. In particular, we will look at some of the smallest things in the Universe.

1

1. What are your thoughts about the size and age of the Universe?
2. People often feel insignificant when they think about these things. Read the following reaction of a writer to his place in the Universe:

"When I consider your heavens, the work of your fingers, the moon and the stars, which you have set in place, what is man that you are mindful of him, the son of man that you care for him?"

(quotation from *Psalm 8*)

3. Who do you think the writer was talking to?
4. Try to rewrite the quotation in your own words.
5. Do you think that we human beings are important in the Universe?

Note

When we are working with very small sizes, it is helpful to write the numbers in standard form. This particularly helps us compare sizes at a glance. For numbers less than "1" we will need to use a **negative power of ten**.

e.g. $2 \times 10^{-3} = 2 \times \frac{1}{1000} = \frac{2}{1000} = 0.002$

How big is "small"?

Read through the following five facts:

- An adult human being has approximately 100 million million **cells** in his/her body.
- Antibiotics are not effective against a **virus**.
- Each one of us has, within our body, ten times as many **bacteria** as we have cells of our own.
- Pondskaters are insects which can stand on the surface of a pond because water molecules attract one another.
- There are more hydrogen **atoms** in the human body than there are atoms of any other type.

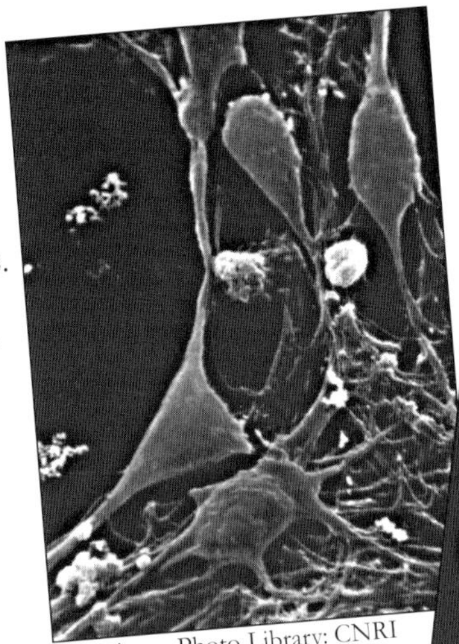
Science Photo Library: CNRI

Left: Nerve cells
Below: Vitamin C molecule

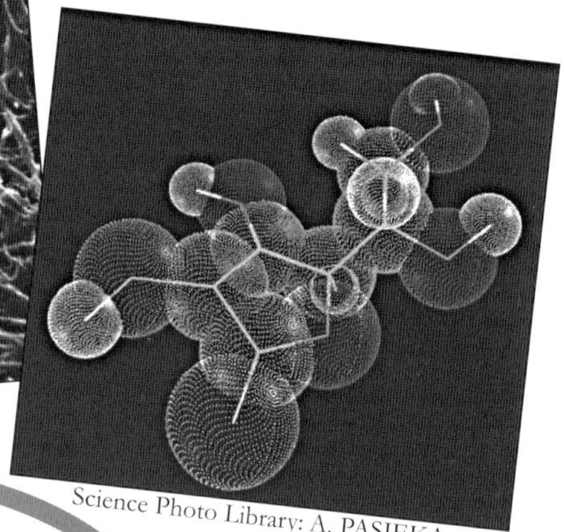
Science Photo Library: A. PASIEKA

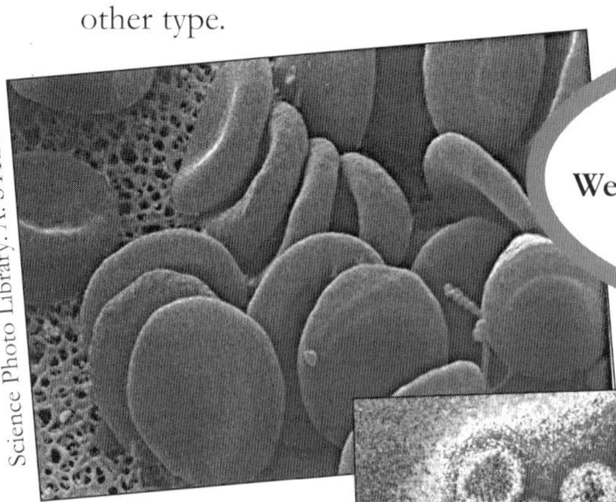
Science Photo Library: A. SYRED

Cells; viruses; bacteria; molecules and atoms. We know they are small, but how small? How do they compare in size?

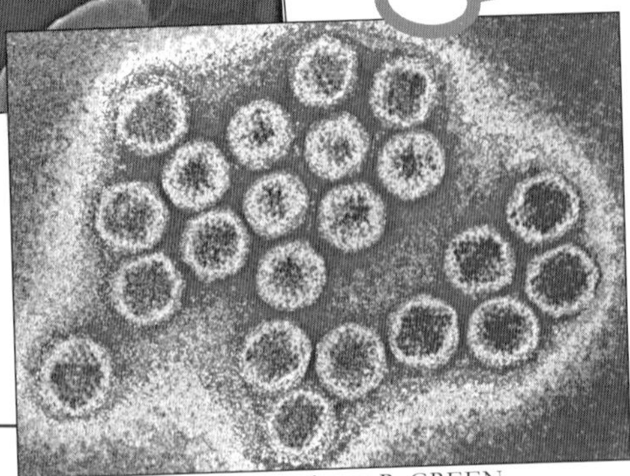
Science Photo Library: R. GREEN

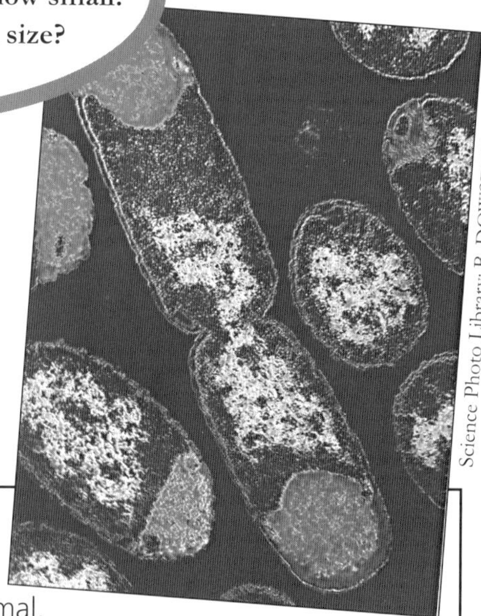
Science Photo Library: B. DOWSETT/CAMR

Above: Red blood cells
Right: Cold viruses
Far right: *E coli* bacteria

2

1. In each part of this question, the numbers are given in standard form. Write each number as an ordinary decimal.
   a) Most cells are about 1×10^{-2} mm across.
   b) Viruses are no bigger than 1×10^{-4} mm across.
   c) Some atoms are only 1×10^{-9} mm across.
   d) A molecule may be as small as 1×10^{-6} mm.
   e) Small bacteria are approximately 1×10^{-3} mm.
2. Using the information in question 1, write the items, cell, virus, molecule, atom, bacteria, in order of size starting with the largest. Then write, next to each item, its size given in standard form.
3. Which item in the list is approximately 100 times bigger than a virus?
4. For each of the following statements, say whether they are true or false:
   a) Atoms are three times larger than bacteria.
   b) Most cells are at least one hundred times bigger than viruses.
   c) If a cell is 1×10^{-2} mm across and a virus is 1×10^{-4} mm, you could fit 100 viruses across a cell.
   d) If a cell is 1×10^{-2} mm across and a bacteria is 1×10^{-3} mm across, the bacteria would not fit into the cell.

Splitting the atom

All livings things are built from cells and the cells are made up of molecules. Molecules can take many different forms because they are made from combinations of atoms, the smallest building block in the Universe.

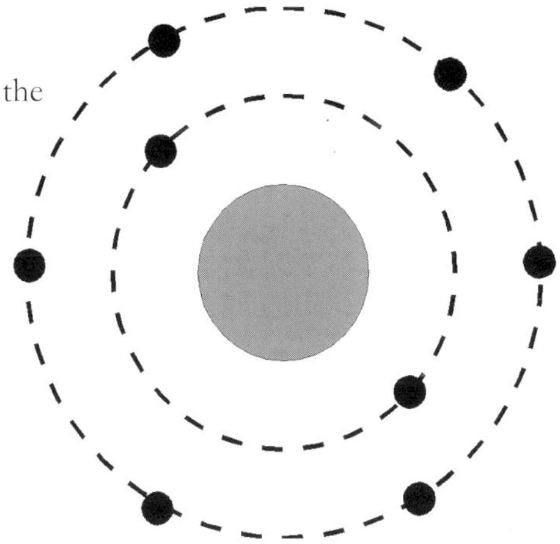

Opposite is a model of an oxygen atom. (It is not drawn to scale).
The solid part in the middle is called the **nucleus** and the small dots round the outside represent **electrons** which move around the nucleus.
Splitting the atom is very difficult and releases huge amounts of energy giving us atomic power and the atom bomb.

The nucleus is made up of protons and neutrons. (In the oxygen atom pictured, there are 8 of each.) These are so small that their masses are always given in standard form.

Rest mass of proton: 1.672×10^{-27} kg
Rest mass of neutron: 1.675×10^{-27} kg
Rest mass of electron: 9.11×10^{-31} kg

3 Use your knowledge of standard form to answer the following questions.

1. a) Which two particles are almost the same size?
   b) Arrange the three particles in order, starting with the smallest.
   c) Roughly how many times heavier is a proton than an electron? Give your answer to the nearest thousand.

2. a) The masses in the table above are given in kg. What would you have to multiply them by in order to change them into grams?
   b) Write each mass in grams in standard form.

3. a) The oxygen nucleus contains 8 protons and 8 neutrons. What would you expect its mass to be? Give your answer in kg and in standard form.
   b) When the protons and the neutrons fuse together into the nucleus some of their rest mass is lost in the effort, so the actual mass of an oxygen nucleus is only 2.655×10^{-26} kg. Compare this with your answer to part a). How much mass has been lost? Give your answer in kg and in standard form.

Exploding stars!

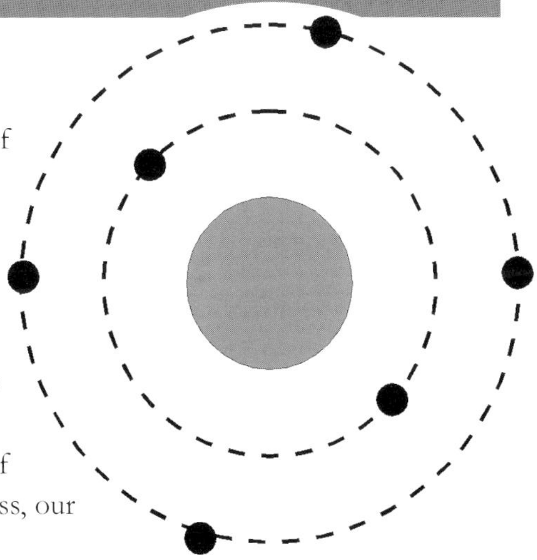

Oxygen is only one of the elements needed to form our bodies. One of the most important is carbon.

A carbon atom is shown opposite.
Carbon atoms can join together to make large molecules that are needed to build our bodies. Carbon was not present in the early Universe, so where did it come from? Most astronomers and physicists believe that carbon is formed deep within stars. Dying stars, called Supernova, explode, scattering carbon into space. Future generations of stars and planets form using this scattered material. Without this process, our bodies could not be created.

4

In this task you will need to use standard form numbers with positive and negative powers of ten.

1. In this question, write any ordinary numbers in standard form and any standard form numbers as ordinary numbers.

   a) Protons and neutrons first appeared when the Universe was only 0.01 seconds old.
   b) After about 200 seconds hydrogen and helium were formed.
   c) At this time, the temperature was about 1×10^9 °K. It had to be 'just right' for the neutrons and protons to fuse successfully.
   d) After about a million years the Universe was cool enough for electrons to attach themselves to nuclei and form atoms.
   e) After about ten million years, gravity caused first generation stars to form.
   f) Nuclear reactions inside these stars formed carbon when the Universe was about ten thousand million years old.

Work in standard form for the rest of these questions, showing all your working.

2. Two million, million, million, million protons would weigh just over a gram. Write this number in standard form and hence work out how many protons would weigh about a kg.

3. When a torch lights up, about 20 billion billion electrons pass through the wire every second. Write this number in standard form and hence calculate the number of electrons passing through the wire in one millisecond.

> **Note**
>
> One billion is one thousand million.
>
> One millisecond is one thousandth of a second.

4. One page of this book is about 2×10^{-2} cm thick. If an atom is 2×10^{-8} cm how many atoms thick is this page?

5. Use the table to answer the questions below

Type of atom	A = number of protons and neutrons
Hydrogen	1
Carbon	12
Oxygen	16

   a) The mass, M, of an atom can be calculated from the following formula:

$$M = A \times 1.66 \times 10^{-27} \text{ kg}$$

   Use the formula to calculate the masses of the three atoms in the table.

   b) The approximate radius, R, of an atom in metres is given by the formula:

$$R = 1.4 \times \sqrt[3]{A} \times 10^{-15}$$

   Use this formula to calculate the radii of the three atoms in the table.

"We are all made from the ashes of dead stars."
John Polkinghorne

So what is the inside story?

So it seems that we can only exist because the Universe is old enough to have produced second generation stars and planets. What is more, many scientists believe that conditions in the early Universe had to be very finely balanced, otherwise things would have happened too quickly, or too slowly for all the elements necessary for life to form.

Professor Paul Davies is an eminent physicist who does not claim any religious faith but his studies of the Universe led him to describe it as

"... a Universe full of stunning surprises."

and he concludes ...

"... it is difficult not to be struck by some of the surprisingly fortuitous accidents without which our existence would be impossible."

So, is our presence here on Earth just some cosmic accident or is it because of a design behind the Universe? What do you think?

What's the time?

UNIT 17

This unit helps students to learn about the background to our present day calendar and about calendars used by people in other places and at other times. It goes on to encourage them to think about their own approaches to time and the uses they make of it.

Using this unit

This unit could be used with students of any tier at GCSE. Some mathematical content may need revision with lower tier students.

It should take about 2 hours, but the length of time will depend on the amount of discussion.

The unit contains several sections all related to the theme of time. There is quite a lot of information so you will need to consider whether you allow students to work independently on the text or whether to present some of the ideas yourself. Each section can lead to class discussion of the issues raised.

Additional sources

A good source on the theory of relativity is *Introducing Einstein's Relativity*, by D'Inverno (OUP, 1992).
A very informative Web site is
http://astro.nmsu.edu/~lhuber/leaphist.html

Students will require a calculator.

Mathematical content

Number (AT2)
- Using calculation skills
- Using negative numbers
- Using large numbers (million/billion)

Algebra (AT2)
(extension activity only)
- Using formulae
- Constructing graphs

Handling data (AT4)
- Calculating mean average

Spiritual and moral development

The aim of this unit is to give students an opportunity to reflect on the nature of time and their use of it and thereby leads into issues of purpose and meaning.

Looking at the way in which non-European societies have developed alternative calendars, it aims to help them to appreciate other views of reality.

TEACHER'S NOTES

Notes on the activities

BC/AD

This section requires students to have some basic understanding of negative numbers. It illustrates the importance of religious belief in the history and culture of a society. All three calendars mentioned are based on an important religious event, as seen by that society. The predominance of Western European culture has made the Christian calendar the standard one, but the others are still used, particularly by religious communities in some other cultures.

A possible discussion point here is the difference between a cyclic calendar – perhaps containing the message that progress is illusory – and a linear one, which suggests that history is going forward.

The details of different calendars can become extremely complicated, and would probably not be worth pursuing in detail.

Leap Years

This section requires students to have some understanding of mean average and decimal fractions. The year 2000 is a Leap Year, although many people think otherwise. The divisible-by-400-and-not-simply-by-100 rule explains this.

It may be worth discussing the extent to which our awareness of the natural environment affects our consciousness of the changing seasons. For some students, the start of the football season in August may be much more significant than harvesting the crops.

Big numbers

This section requires students to have some understanding of large numbers, such as a million and a billion. A second is sufficiently small - but still perceptible- that we can use it to gauge the meaning of some very large numbers.

The time of your life?

This section requires students to calculate fractions of quantities and to know how to construct a pie chart. The paradox could lead to a discussion of Venn diagrams and the importance of not counting the intersection of two sets twice.

Science and time (extension activity)

This section is for extension work at higher level.

It requires students to use a complex formula and to interpret graphical information.

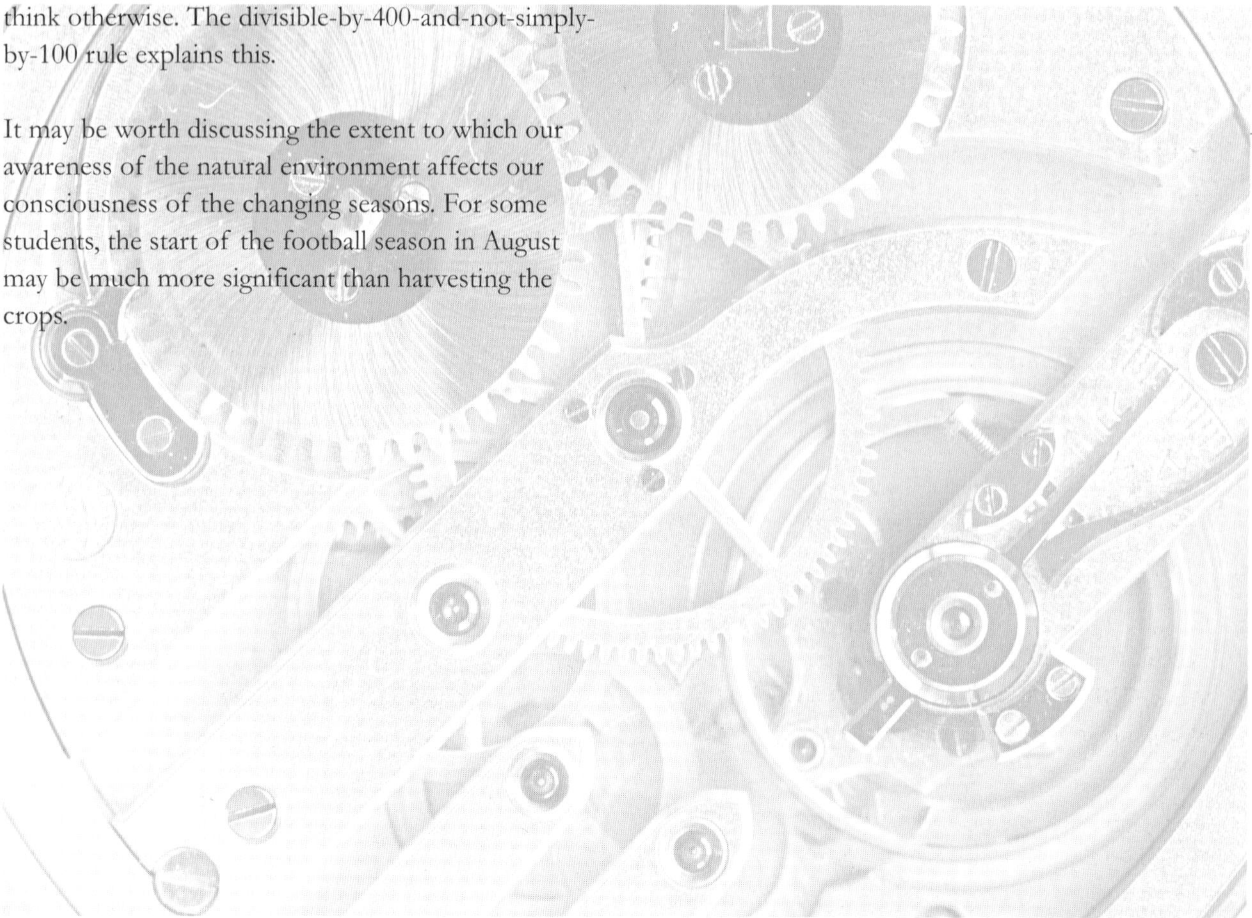

Answers

(Some questions are for discussion with no prescribed answers)

1. BC/AD

1. Because it is regarded as a very important event.
2. In the year that we call 44 BC, the coin minters could hardly have known that Jesus would be born 44 years later!
3.

Event	Date in Christian calendar	Date in Jewish calendar	Date in Muslim calendar
Creation	3761 BC	0	- 4341
Birth of Christ	0	3761	- 580
Mohammed flees from Mecca	580	4341	0
Battle of Hastings	1066	4837	486
Yom Kippur War	1973	5734	1393

4. Religious events were regarded as the most important events in history, particularly when calendars were being instituted. It may be worth while asking what event would society use today?
5. Clearly the Christian calendar predominates throughout the world, and is the *de facto* standard. The others are still used in their own communities.
6. The original Roman year had ten months. This was changed to 12 months (based on the lunar cycle) with the insertion of July and August (named after Julius Caesar and Augustus Caesar). This meant that September, October, November and December, formerly the 7th, 8th, 9th and 10th months became the 9th, 10th, 11th and 12th months.

2. Leap Years

1. It would be 0.24219 days or 5 hours 49 minutes.
2. After 100 years, 24.219 days; after 700 years, about 6 months.
4. Caesar: error is 0.00781 days, or 11.2 minutes.
5. After 1500 years, error is 12 days.
7. Gregorian: in 400 years, get 97 leap years and 303 normal years, so the total number of days in 400 years is 303 x 365 + 9 7x 366 = 146097, and the average length of the year is then 146097/400 = 365.2425.
8. Alternative system would give (304 x 365 + 96 x 366)/400 = 146096/400 = 365.24
9. The current error is 0.00031 days per year, or 27 seconds per year. After 10,000 years, there will still be an error of only 3.1 days.

3. Big numbers

1. a) 11 days 14 hours.
   b) 31.7 years.
2. 2.2 billion seconds.
3. 60 billion seconds.

4. The time of your life?

1. 48 years, 24 years, 3.4 years, 0.4 years left for work!

5. Science and time

1. 0.9999999992.
2. Graph:

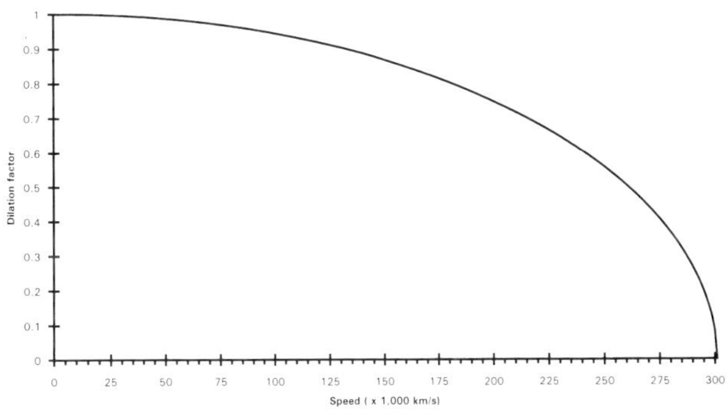

3. (The following answers are obtained by calculation rather than from the graph.)
   a) (i) 259,808 km/s.
      (ii) 298,496 km/s.
      (iii) 299,985 km/s.
   b) (i) 10.01 years.
      (ii) 20.02 years.
      (iii) Dilation factor is 0.0447.
      (iv) 0.895 years i.e. 11 months.

What's the time?

UNIT 17

The Millennium year, 2000 AD, has generated lots of excitement and interest. It reminds us of the importance of time and dates. It is interesting to see how time is measured, and to reflect on how much we appreciate and value the time we have.

BC/AD

1

1. Most countries in the Western world measure the year from the supposed birth date of Jesus Christ. Why do you think they do this?

2. An archaeologist dug up a coin inscribed 'Julius Caesar 44 BC'. How did she know it was a fake?

info

In fact, several hundred years after this system started, it was realised that there had been a mistake in calculating the year in which Christ was born. It is now thought that he was probably born in 6 BC but it would be too complicated to change the world's calendars!

Other cultures use different starting points for their calendars. It is well known that the Chinese name their years after animals – the Year of the Dog etc. When they have gone through the list of animals, they then repeat the sequence, so theirs is a *cyclic calendar*.

Jewish people count from 3761 years before Christ, so they are now in the year 5757. Their starting point is the time at which they suppose the world was created.

Muslims measure from 580 years after the birth of Christ, when Mohammed fled from Mecca. So for them, the year 2000 AD is 1420.

3. Complete the following table

Event	Date in Christian calendar	Date in Jewish calendar	Date in Muslim calendar
Creation		0	
Birth of Christ	0		
Mohammed flees from Mecca			0
Battle of Hastings	1066		
Yom Kippur War		5734	

1

Task 1 continued

4. What sort of event is the basis for all of these calendars? Why is this?

5. Do you think it would be better if all countries agreed on the same year numbering method? If so, which one should they use? Why?

info

Different cultures also have different ways of dividing the year up. The Western world uses 12 months of slightly different lengths. The names of these months are interesting, reflecting their origin in the Roman civilization; so, for example, October is literally the eighth month, and December is the tenth.

6. Investigate why October is not our eighth month now.

info

In the Muslim calendar, months have 29 and 30 days alternately. This means that after 12 months have passed and the first one starts again, less than a year has passed. This is why religious feasts like Ramadhan move forward 11 days each year – in 1992 it was in April and in 1996 it was in February.

Leap Years

A year is the time the earth takes to go exactly once around the sun. Unfortunately, this is not a whole number of days. In fact, it takes 365.24219 days, as accurately as we can measure it.

2

1. If we took each year to be exactly 365 days, what would the error be? What is this in hours?

2. The error may seem small, but it would accumulate. What would it be after 100 years? After 700 years?

!

This would mean that, after 100 years, when it should be, say, June, the weather would be a month 'behind', and it would feel like May. After about 700 years, there would be a slippage of 6 months, so on December 25th, Christmas Day, we would be enjoying hot sunshine, and barbecuing the turkey – just as they now do in Australia!

To avoid this problem, and to keep the different calendar dates at the same time of the 'weather year', people have introduced simple modifications to the basic idea of 365-day years.

2

Task 2 continued

info

The first change was made by Julius Caesar in 46 BC (he didn't know it was BC, as we've seen already!). The standard 365-day calendar had been started several hundred years earlier, and there was already a slippage of about 3 months. To remedy this, Caesar invented Leap Years.

He ordered that every fourth year should have an extra day. This means that in every cycle of four years, the total number of days is

$$3 \times 365 + 1 \times 366$$

This comes to 1461 days. If we average this over the four years, we get a mean length of 365.25 days.

This is clearly very close to the correct value, and so this system was used for almost 1600 years. It is called the Julian calendar.

There are other ways of getting an average near 365.24219 days. For example, suppose there were 8 leap years in every cycle of 33 years. The total number of days in the cycle would be

$$25 \times 365 + 8 \times 366 = 12{,}053$$

If we average this over 33 years, we get 12053/33 = 365.242424... This is an even better result, but it would be difficult to remember which years were leap years!

3. Can you invent other leap year systems which would give an average year length near to 365.24219?

4. Calculate the difference between the average under Caesar's system, 365.25 days, and the best measured value at present, 365.24219 days
   a) in days, b) in minutes.

5. Over many years, the error in the Julian calendar will again build up. What is the accumulated error after 1500 years?

info

A slippage of almost 12 days was beginning to become noticeable. To solve this difficulty, a further modification was made: century years (although divisible by 4) would only be leap years if they were divisible by 400. So, for example, 1600 and 2000 are leap years, but 1700, 1800 and 1900 aren't. This system was introduced by Pope Gregory in 1582 on the continent, but not until 1752 in Britain. By that time, the calendar was 12 days out, and so it was decided by the government that September 2nd should be followed by September 14th. This apparent loss of 12 days caused serious rioting in many parts of the country – people thought that they were losing twelve days of their lives.

We can see that people were not losing part of their lives – it was just a re-labelling of the days of their lives. However, their reaction can make us think about the importance of time in our own lives.

2

Task 2 continued

6. Suppose you really did lose 12 days from your life – perhaps in a coma after a road accident. Would you feel very upset about the lost time? Some people might feel most upset because they had missed episodes from their favourite soap on TV; others because of the things that they have not been able to do in the lost time. What would you miss most?

info

The calendar devised by Pope Gregory means that on a cycle now of 400 years, instead of 100 leap years and 300 normal years, there are now 97 leap years and 303 normal years.

7. How many days does this give in each complete cycle of 400 years? What is the average length of a year?

8. What would the average be if the '400 years' were like the other century years, and not leap years?

9. Calculate the error in the current Gregorian system. How much would it amount to after 10,000 years?

10. In previous times, it was important to know about the seasons of the year. Nowadays, most of us are much more cut off from agriculture and the natural world. We don't know much about the lambing season, or about harvest time. Do you think that this lack of awareness of our natural environment matters?

In other societies e.g. Iran, the slippage of the seasons relative to the calendar is tolerated. Do you think we should be so bothered about it? Would it matter if we had Christmas in the hottest time of the year?

Big numbers

Most of us are not very good at imagining what a million or a billion is really like – how big is it? One easy way to get some idea of what these huge numbers mean is to find out how many seconds there are in various periods of time.

For example, how many seconds are there in a year? There are 60 seconds in a minute, 60 minutes in an hour, 24 hours in a day, 365 days in a (normal) year. This gives 60 x 60 x 24 x 365 = 31,536,000 seconds in a year.

3

1. From this result, estimate roughly how long
   a) one million seconds lasts (give your answer in days);
   b) one billion seconds lasts (i.e. one thousand million seconds), (give your answer in years).

2. How long, in seconds, can you expect to live?

3. How long, in seconds, is it since 0 BC?

The time of your life?

It can be surprising to consider how you are going to spend all the time of your life.

4

Firstly, a paradox:

1. Suppose you live for 72 years (about average, and a nice number for division!). About one third of your life is spent sleeping. After taking that away, how long does it leave you with?

   Another third is spent in leisure activities, between sleeping and working. How much does that leave?

   2/7 of your 72 years is spent in weekends. What is left now?

   Take an hour each day for eating – 1/24th of your life. How much time is finally left for work? Where is the catch?

2. Do a class survey on how much time, on average, each week is spent at school; eating; sleeping; travelling; being with friends.

   Illustrate the results with a pie-chart.

Do you think that you spend your time well?

Do you waste a lot of it?

Are there things that you wish you had done instead?

How good are you at telling the time? As an exercise for the whole class, close your eyes and put your hand up when you think one minute has passed. Your teacher will tell you who got closest.

'Time flies when you're enjoying yourself' – which lessons seem to last the longest?

When 3-year-old children are told to wait for 5 minutes, it can make them very impatient. For a 15-year-old, a similar request is more easily tolerated. Is this because 5 minutes is a bigger fraction of life for the 3-year-old than for the 15-year-old? How much bigger?

Similarly, for a 40-year-old, the previous year in his or her life represents a fairly small fraction (one fortieth) of the total, but for a 5-year-old, the previous year is one fifth of his whole life so far. This can give a different perspective on time and the way we use it. It can make the experiences we have in the first years of our lives more significant than those in later life.

Not many of us know when we are going to die, and so we cannot count off the days until that event. However, convicts sentenced to death do know the precise hour, and this can give us some insight into our approach to time, and into what things in life are most important to us.

Suppose you knew that you were going to be executed in exactly one week from now.

What would you do in the last week of your life?

What would you do in the last hour?

This theme has been explored in *The Chamber* by John Grisham, and the film *Dead man walking*.

Science and time

One of the great surprises of modern science is Einstein's discovery that for someone moving at a certain speed v, relative to us, the rate at which their clocks measure time is related to our clocks by a multiple

$$\sqrt{1-(v/c)^2}$$

where c is the speed of light, about 300,000 km/second. This is called the *time dilation factor.*

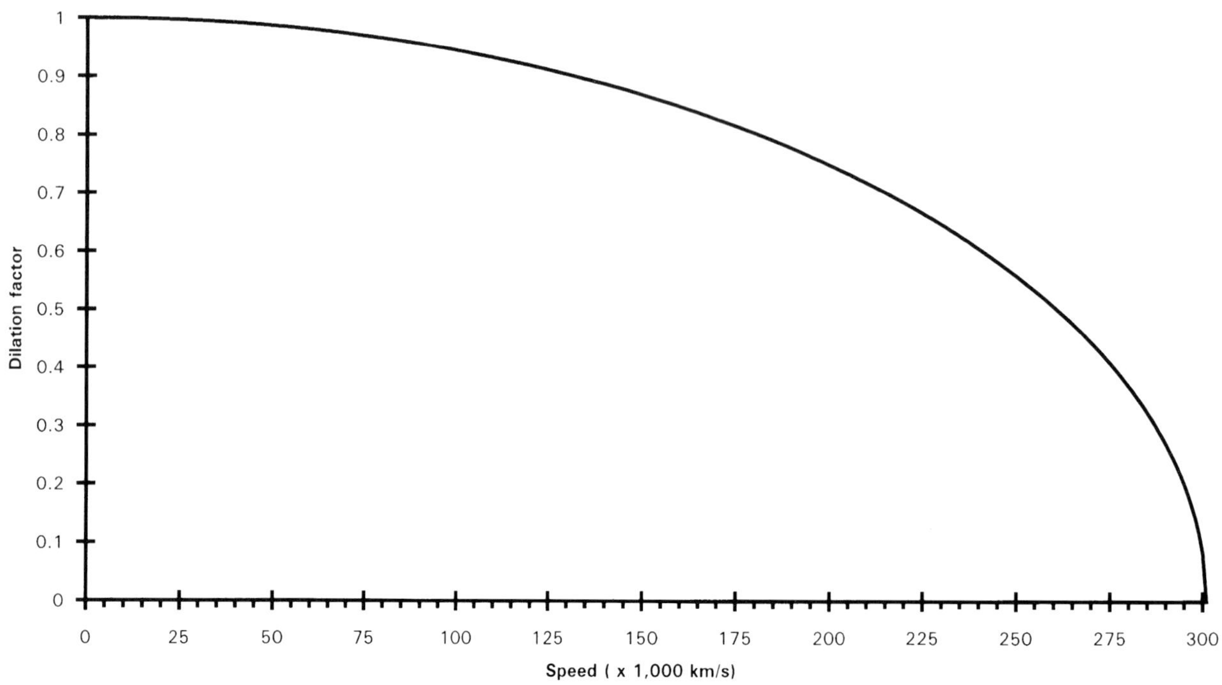

5

1. The fastest any human has ever travelled is about 12 km/sec (astronauts returning from the moon). Work out their time dilation factor.

info

It is clear that this factor is very close to 1 for any reasonable human speed. However, scientists have accelerated very small particles, such as electrons and protons, to very high speeds, and for the particles it does indeed seem that time goes slower.

2. Plot a graph of the time dilation factor for speeds from 0 to 300,000 km/sec.

3. Use the graph to answer these questions:
   a) How fast should you go for time to pass at
      (i) half the normal rate;
      (ii) one tenth of the normal rate; and
      (iii) one hundredth of the normal rate.
   b) Suppose the crew of the Starship Enterprise travel at 0.999c
      (i) How long would they take to get to a nearby star 10 light years away? (A light year is the distance travelled by light in one year).
      (ii) If they turned round and came straight home again, how much time would have passed on earth during their voyage?
      (iii) Calculate their time dilation factor.
      (iv) How much older would the crew be when they returned?

This effect has caused much bewilderment but it seems to be fully confirmed by atomic experiments. We will have to wait a long time before testing it on humans!

The way that time passes is a great mystery. We can't manipulate it or use it, but simply have to go with it.

Why, for example, can we remember the past but not the future?

Why does time only seem to go in one direction?

Why can't we travel back in time?

!

Time travel is very popular in science fiction stories, but it raises deep logical problems. Suppose that you could travel back into the past, and that you then chose to kill your great-grand parents whilst they were still children.

What would be the consequences of this?!

Many scientists, philosophers and theologians think that time is something that was created as part of the universe, and that God the creator is not in time. Somehow, he is like the author of a novel, who is not in the same time-sequence as the characters he is writing about. This is extremely difficult to imagine! As beings in time, we cannot easily envisage a situation in which time does not exist.

Could it be YOU?

UNIT 18

In this unit, students use number and data handling skills within the context of the national lottery. They are also encouraged to examine the motivation of people who participate in the lottery and consider what this tells them about different priorities in life.

Using this unit

This unit is accessible for all students at GCSE level. It is expected that this unit would take about 3 hours, plus the time for collecting data using a prepared questionnaire.

As a preliminary activity, students are asked to use a questionnaire to do a survey on various aspects of the national lottery. This questionnaire will need to be issued at least two lessons prior to starting the unit. This is because it is necessary to collate the results before other work can begin. The beginning and concluding sections encourage students to consider why so many people take part in the lottery. Also, throughout the unit there are statements which offer opportunities for further reflection.

The central sections examine how much people spend on the lottery, where the money goes, the idea of luck and the probability of winning. There is also an optional extension activity, which is more suitable for Intermediate/Higher tier students. This leads students through the process of calculating the probability of a jackpot.

It is hoped that the unit will encourage students to examine both the positive attributes and the possible dangers of the lottery. Sensitivity may be needed if students are asked to take the questionnaire home. Some parents may not wish to take part in the survey.

Students will require a scientific calculator with a factorial button.

Mathematical content

Number & Algebra (AT2)
- Calculate percentages
- Explore number patterns
- Understand and use factorials
- Calculate combinations

Handling data (AT4)
- Interpret information from tables
- Use a questionnaire to collect data
- Identify all the possible outcomes
- Calculate a probability based on equally likely outcomes
- Recognise that the total probability of all mutually exclusive outcomes is 1

Spiritual and moral development

It is hoped that students will reflect upon what is important to them in life, when considering the advantages and disadvantages of the national lottery. They are also encouraged to consider the extent to which they believe life is governed by chance.

TEACHER'S NOTES

Background

The National Lottery Act was passed by Parliament in 1993, enabling a national lottery to be set up in the UK. The Camelot consortium, one of eight consortia, was awarded the licence. Camelot outlined a plan that would maximise sales whilst retaining the lowest percentage of sales income to cover all operating costs, including profits. The first draw took place on 19th November 1994. Anyone aged 16 or over can take part.

Since then the lottery has gone from strength to strength. Most of the adult population of the UK have played in the lottery with an estimated 65% of the population playing regularly. In early 1997, a new midweek draw held on a Wednesday was started.

Further free information including the "rules of play" can be obtained from Camelot at the address given below.

Additional sources

Available from Camelot are:
The National Lottery Fact Pack
Rules For On-Line Games And The National Lottery Game Procedures 2nd Edition
Fact sheet on National Lottery winning numbers and draw results

Camelot Group Plc., The National Lottery, PO. Box 287, Watford, Herts, WD1 8TT

Notes on the activities

National Lottery Questionnaire

This is a preliminary activity, which must be completed before starting on the other tasks in the unit. The students should all use at least one questionnaire, possibly with their own household. However, if possible, further adults could also be interviewed. The questionnaires should then be processed and the results summarised. Students will need their own questionnaire back as well as a copy of the class results, when they are doing the unit.

Why play the lottery?

After a brief account of the national lottery in Britain students work through a short exercise on marketing the national lottery. They are asked to think up their own slogan.

Class discussion

There is scope for class discussion throughout the unit. It would be particularly beneficial for the introductory session to include a class discussion on the issues raised. It will then set the scene for the rest of the unit. Areas for discussion include:

- the ways in which people were encouraged to play the lottery;
- the students' ideas for marketing the lottery;
- their own views on the positive and negative aspects of the lottery.

"It's only a pound!"

Students calculate how much money is spent on the national lottery in Britain and, using results from their class survey, how much is spent by families in their own neighbourhood. Students should be encouraged to reflect on whether this is a good way to spend the money in light of the needs of the local community.

Where does all the money go?

In this section, students look at where each pound that is used to buy a ticket goes and whether they think this is a fair distribution. They should be given an opportunity to compare their ideas with those of others in the class. This might include reviewing who should benefit most from the lottery and the value of the prizes.

Lucky numbers

In this section, students examine whether in reality there are certain numbers which are "lucky" for people and whether or not choosing the same numbers each time or choosing the numbers at random has any effect on chances of winning. They will need to appreciate the difference between the theoretical and the practical in probability, when considering the data provided. Students are then encouraged to think more generally about the idea of being lucky and what it is based upon.

It's all a matter of chance

In this section, students consider the probabilities of winning the different prizes. (Note: It is at this point that the optional extension activity *What chance a jackpot?* can be used.) This section aims to highlight the fact that even though the chance of winning the jackpot is very small, the idea that "it could be me" operates as a significant driving force in people's participation.

Note that in this section on different probabilities the word *chance* has been used. This is because this word ties in better with common understanding of the lottery. Students should be made aware of this in relation to their understanding of probability in order that there is no confusion.

Finally in this section, students are encouraged to think whether or not our lives and the events that take place in our lives are based purely on chance or whether there may be other forces at work.

What are we hoping for?

In this final section, students should be encouraged to think again about the possible motivations for playing the lottery. This then leads on to further reflection of what people hope for in their lives and whether the lottery can provide it. Students could be asked to produce a written response either as preparation for or as a result of a final class discussion.

Class discussion

There are a fair number of issues raised by this unit and a final class discussion is important in order to draw the threads together. In particular, the following could be addressed:

- the students' views on why people play the lottery;
- the students' views on what people are really hoping for through the lottery.

What chance a jackpot? (extension activity)

This activity can be used just as students are starting the *It's all a matter of chance* activity. In this extension activity, students are led through a process that leads to calculating the probability of the national lottery jackpot. The first stage requires students to list all possible outcomes and then the associated probabilities in some simple lotteries. This is followed by using Pascal's triangle to find the number of possible winning combinations. Finally, the students are introduced to the formula for calculating combinations. Some of the mathematics is beyond GCSE but it is worthwhile leading students through it.

Answers

Task 2:

1. 30 million.
2. a) £70.5 million, b) £122.20.

Task 5:

1. a) less than a chance in a million.
2. a) 0.018, b) 2%.
3. Possible answer is guessing correctly a playing card selected at random from a normal pack.
4. a) 53/54, b) 98%.

Task 6:

1. a)

1,2	1,3	1,4	1,5	1,6	1,7	2,3	2,4	2,5	2,6	2,7
3,4	3,5	3,6	3,7	4,5	4,6	4,7	5,6	5,7	6,7	

b) 21 possibilities, c) 1/21, d) 1/21.

2. a)

1,2,3	1,2,4	1,2,5	1,2,6	1,2,7	1,3,4	1,3,5	1,3,6	1,3,7	1,4,5	1,4,6
1,4,7	1,5,6	1,5,7	1,6,7	2,3,	2,3,5	2,3,6	2,3,7	2,4,5	2,4,6	2,4,7
2,5,6	2,5,7	2,6,7	3,4,5	3,4,6	3,4,7	3,5,6	3,5,7	3,6,7	4,5,6	4,5,7
4,6,7	5,6,7									

b) 35 different choices, c) 1/35.

Task 7:

2. 56 possible choices.
3. 1/15.
4. a) This can include patterns in rows, columns and diagonals
   b)

Row 9	9	36	84	126	126	84	36	9	1	
Row 10	10	45	120	210	252	210	120	45	10	1

Task 8:

1. a) 210, b) 26334.
2. a) 1/220, b) 1/4845.
3. b) 13983816, c) 1/13983816.

Could it be YOU?

UNIT 18

Why play the lottery?

National lotteries take place in quite a few countries around the world. In Britain, the national lottery began in 1994. From the time it started, it has been extremely popular and most adults have played at least once. Many play regularly and it is estimated that as many as 65% of all adults play every week. In other words, nearly 2 out of every 3 adults take part in the lottery each week.

When the lottery was starting in Britain some of the reasons given to people in order to encourage them to take part were:

- It would be **fun** to take part.
- They might end up with millions of pounds to **spend** on themselves.
- The **chance** of winning millions of pounds is the same for everyone so it might as well be them.
- Millions of pounds would be given to **good causes.**
- The **moment of winning**, when they discover they have won millions of pounds, would be the most exciting moment of their lives.

1

1. Why do you think so many people take part in the lottery?
2. What do you think is the main attraction?
3. Imagine you were setting up a national lottery in a country for the first time. What would your slogan be?

The slogan used to promote the British national lottery was

'It could be you!'

What do you think – could it be you?

"It's only a pound!"

It costs £1 to buy a ticket for the lottery. Some people say, "It's only a pound – that's not much to spend, really". In this section you will examine how much is spent by people on the lottery. You will need your results from the National Lottery Questionnaires that you completed earlier.

2

1. If the number of adults in Britain is 45 million and nearly 2 out of every 3 adults play every week, approximately how many people are playing?

2. Each player spends on average £2.35 a week on the lottery.
   a) How much money is spent altogether in Britain each week on the lottery?
   b) How much does each player spend on average in a year on the lottery in Britain?
   c) Do you think this is money well spent?
   d) What sort of things could that money have been spent on instead?

3. a) How much is spent in your home every week on the lottery?
   b) How much is that over a whole year?
   c) Is this higher or lower than the national average?

4. a) Work out the total amount spent each week by the families surveyed by your class.
   b) Work out the total amount spent each year by these families.
   c) Work out the average amount spent each week by the families surveyed by your class.
   d) What is the average amount for the year?

5. a) Do you think this is money well spent or are there other things this money could have been spent on in your area?
   b) Are the average figures for your class higher or lower than the national figures?
   c) Can you think of any reasons why this might be the case?
   d) What is the highest amount spent by any one person?

6. a) How many families have lost more money than they have won?
   b) What percentage is this of all the families surveyed?
   c) Is this a higher or lower percentage than you would expect?

Can you imagine what it would be like to win a big jackpot prize?

In what ways do you think it would change your life?

Where does all the money go?

So what happens to all the money that is spent on lottery tickets? Some of the money goes towards the prize money. Some has to be paid to various people including the Government Treasury, the shop where you play (Retailer), and the organisers for their operating costs and profit. The rest goes towards good causes such as the arts, sports, charities, National Heritage and the Millennium Fund. The table below shows how the current organisers distribute every pound spent on the lottery.

Prize Money	50p
Treasury Duty	12p
Good Causes	28p
Retailer Commission	5p
Operating costs & profit	5p
Total	**£1**

The treasury duty is a fixed amount and cannot be changed from 12p.

3

1. Which of the five sections in the table would you give most to?
2. Which section would you give least to?
3. Write down how much you would give each area.
4. Ask one or two of your friends how they would split up each pound. Write down what they say.

Lucky numbers

Many people when selecting their six numbers choose the same numbers each time. They might use their house number or the day of the month they were born on. These numbers are often considered to be "lucky." The table below shows how many times each number appeared during the first 50 lottery draws.

Number	1	2	3	4	5	6	7	8	9	10	11	12	13
Times drawn	7	8	8	7	15	6	6	7	5	8	6	6	5
Number	14	15	16	17	18	19	20	21	22	23	24	25	26
Times drawn	6	11	12	8	6	5	5	8	12	4	6	9	6
Number	27	28	29	30	31	32	33	34	35	36	37	38	39
Times drawn	5	8	6	10	9	7	5	6	5	6	5	9	1
Number	40	41	42	43	44	45	46	47	48	49			
Times drawn	7	8	7	7	10	8	8	7	8	6			

4

1. Using the results from your questionnaires, work out what percentage of families in your class select the same numbers most of the time.
2. What sort of reasons did people give for saying that some numbers were "lucky" for them?
3. For the families surveyed by your class, did those who used "lucky" numbers do any better than those who chose any numbers? Explain how you work out your answer.
4. Do you think that some numbers are more "lucky" than others and so more likely to come up?
5. Do the results of the first 50 draws surprise you or are they what you would have expected? Explain your answer.

Are some people especially lucky or unlucky in life?

If you think they are, can you explain why you think this?

It's all a matter of chance

In Britain it was found that chance was the most appealing reason for people wanting to take part in the lottery. The idea that "someone has to win the jackpot so it might as well be me" was considered the most important reason why people might want to take part. It was therefore decided to make this the main issue when advertising the lottery. Outside every shop selling tickets and on every advertisement is the slogan "It could be You".

To take part in the lottery you choose six numbers between 1 and 49. To win the jackpot (usually worth millions of pounds) you have to get all the six numbers correct. (To work out the chance of getting all six numbers correct is quite complex. Your teacher may ask you to do this by using the "What chance a jackpot?" sheet).

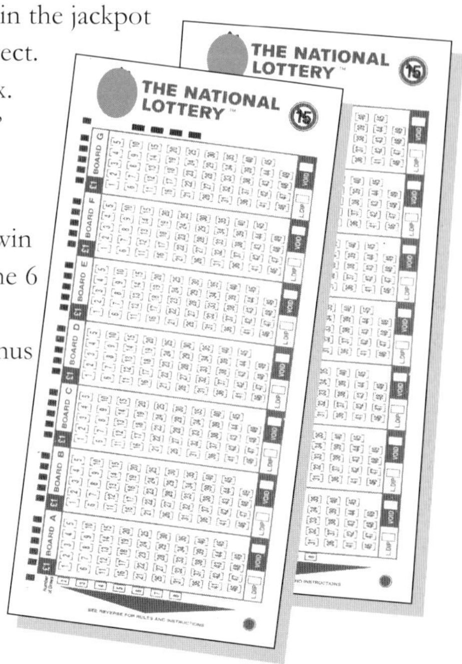

Of course you don't have to get all 6 of your numbers correct in order to win a prize. The smallest prize is £10 and is won if you have chosen three of the 6 numbers selected. The chance of winning £10 is 1 in 57. There are other larger prizes for getting 4 or 5 of your numbers correct. There is also a Bonus Number which may be used when people get 5 numbers out of their six correct. The prize money for these categories is not fixed but depends on the number of people who have played.

The table on the next page shows the chances of winning each prize category. We are using the word "chance" here. This is really the same as "probability" which you may be more used to using in mathematics.

Match 3 out of 6 (£10 prize)	1 / 57
Match 4 out of 6	1 / 1033
Match 5 out of 6	1 / 55,492
Match 5 out of 6 plus the Bonus number	1 / 2,330,636
Match 6 out of 6 (Jackpot)	1 / 13,983,816
The chance of winning any sort of prize	1 / 54

5

1. You may have heard of the phrase "A chance in a million".
   a) Is the chance of winning the jackpot on the lottery more or less than "A chance in a million"?
   b) What do you think now of the slogan used in advertising the lottery –

"It could be You!"?

2. Look at the chance of winning the £10 prize.
   a) Write this chance as a decimal.
   b) Write it as a percentage probability.

3. Look at the overall chance of winning any of the prizes. Can you think of anything else that has a chance of about 1 / 54.

4. a) What is the chance that you will not win a prize at all in any one week?
   b) Write this as a percentage probability.

There are many ways of looking at life.
How do you react to these two different viewpoints?

"Life is a lottery – everything that happens to me in life is just chance."

"I know the plans I have for you," declares the Lord, "plans to prosper you and not to harm you, plans to give you hope and a future." (quotation from the *Bible*)

Just a bit of fun?

What are we hoping for?

The lottery in Britain is certainly proving to be popular, so much so that a Wednesday draw was introduced early in 1997. Having considered in the unit different aspects of the lottery, you are now asked to think about the questions below.

What do you think really drives people to take part in the lottery?

Is it just a bit of fun?

Is it because money goes to good causes?

Is it because people think that they have a good chance of winning some kind of a prize?

Is it because people hope that they might win the jackpot and so their lives will change for the better?

What are you hoping for from life?

What is important to you?

How do these compare to winning the lottery?

Write your response to these questions in preparation for a class discussion.

What chance a jackpot? (extension activity)

You are going to work out the chance of winning the jackpot in the British national lottery. This is quite complex so you will do it in several stages. You will start by considering some simpler lotteries.

Imagine a lottery in which you have just the numbers 1 to 5 to choose from. In this lottery you have to pick just 2 out of the 5 numbers. There are 10 different ways you could choose 2 of those numbers:

1,2 1,3 1,4 1,5 2,3 2,4 2,5 3,4 3,5 4,5

It does not matter in which order the numbers are picked, because in the lottery 1 followed by 2 would be considered the same as 2 followed by 1. Each of the possible choices is equally likely to be selected, so the chance (or probability) of having the winning numbers is 1/(the total number of possible choices). So the chance of winning the jackpot in this simple lottery is $^1/_{10}$.

6

1. Imagine a lottery with the numbers 1 to 7 where you have to choose two numbers.
   a) Write down all your possible choices. The list has been started for you:

   1,2 1,3 1,4 1,5 1,6 1,7 2,3 2,4

   b) How many different possibilities are there?
   c) What is the chance of (2,5) being the winning numbers?
   d) What is the chance of (1,3) being the winning numbers?

2. Now imagine the lottery still with the numbers 1 to 7 but where you have to choose three numbers.
   a) Write down all your possible choices. Again the list has been started for you:

   1,2,3 1,2,4 1,2,5 1,2,6 1,2,7 1,3,4 1,3,5 1,3,6
   1,3,7 1,4,5 1,4,6, 1,4,7 1,5,6 1,5,7 1,6,7 2,3,4
   2,3,5 2,3,6

   b) How many different choices are there altogether?
   c) What is the chance that the 3 numbers you choose are the winning numbers?

Look at this table. The pattern of numbers in this table is very important and has many applications. The number pattern is often called Pascal's Triangle.

	Column 1	Column 2	Column 3	Column 4	Column 5	Column 6	Column 7	Column 8
Row 1	1							
Row 2	2	1						
Row 3	3	3	1					
Row 4	4	6	4	1				
Row 5	5	10	10	5	1			
Row 6	6	15	20	15	6	1		
Row 7	7	21	35	35	21	7	1	
Row 8	8	28	56	70	56	28	8	1

We can use Pascal's Triangle to find the total number of choices there are for different lotteries. For example, consider our simple lottery with 5 numbers where we have to choose 2. The total number of choices is found in Row 5, Column 2. The number there is 10, which is what we found before.

7

1. We can use the table to check the answers we got in task 6.
   a) Check your answer to 1b). Is it correct?
   b) Check your answer to 2b). Is it correct?

2. Imagine a lottery with numbers 1 to 8 where you choose 3 numbers. How many possible choices are there?

3. Imagine a lottery with numbers 1 to 6 where you choose 2 numbers. What is the chance that your choice will be the winning numbers?

4. a) What patterns can you see in the table?
   b) Using the patterns you have found, try to write down the next two rows in the table.
   c) See if you can find a copy of Pascal's Triangle to see how the numbers continue.

Note

6! is read "6 **factorial**".
6! means 6 x 5 x 4 x 3 x 2 x 1
so 6! = 720

8! means 8 x 7 x 6 x 5 x 4 x 3 x 2 x 1
so 8! = 40,320

When calculating the factorial for larger numbers, it is best to use the ! button, which you should find on most scientific calculators.

The number of ways of choosing 2 numbers from 5 can be written as $^5C_2$. The letter C is used to stand for **combinations**. In general, the number of ways (or combinations) of selecting r numbers from n is ^nC_r
There is a formula for working out the number of combinations.

$$^nC_r = \frac{n!}{(n-r)!r!}$$

For example:

$$^5C_2 = \frac{5!}{(5-2)! \times 2!} = \frac{5!}{3! \times 2!} = \frac{5 \times 4 \times 3 \times 2 \times 1}{(3 \times 2 \times 1) \times (2 \times 1)} = \frac{120}{6 \times 2} = 10$$

This means that we can now work out the number of combinations there are without having to write them all out or using Pascal's Triangle.

8

1. Work out how many possible choices there are in the following lotteries where you
   a) choose 4 numbers from 1 to 10;
   b) choose 5 numbers from 1 to 22.

2. Work out the chance of winning the jackpot in the following lotteries where you
   a) choose 3 numbers from 12;
   b) choose 4 numbers from 20.
   c) How small would you describe the chance of a jackpot as in lottery b) ?

3. Do you know roughly what the chance is of winning the national lottery jackpot?
   a) Write it down. Have a guess if you don't know.
   b) How many ways are there of choosing 6 numbers from 1 to 49.
   c) What is the chance of winning the jackpot in the national lottery?

!

If you go and buy a lottery ticket on a Saturday morning, the chance of you dying by the time the draw takes place in the evening is greater than the chance of you winning the Jackpot.

National Lottery Questionnaire

We are doing research on the national lottery and examining the impact it has on society. We would be grateful if you could take some time to answer the following questions.

1. How often do you play the national lottery? Please tick just one of the boxes below:

   Never ☐

   Occasionally (less than once a month) ☐

   Regularly (more than once a month) ☐

   Every Week ☐

2. If you never play, please state the reason why you have decided not to play. You may then ignore the rest of the questionnaire.

   ____

   ____

3. If you do play, how much do you spend on average, to the nearest pound, per week on the national lottery?

   Average spent each week ____________________

4. Since the lottery began have you lost more money than you have won? Yes ☐ No ☐

5. Do you usually select the same six numbers each time you play? Yes ☐ No ☐

6. Do you have "lucky numbers"? Yes ☐ No ☐

   If yes, write down the reason you think they are "lucky".

   ____

   ____

7. What would you say is your main reason for taking part in the national lottery?

   ____

   ____

Thank you for taking part in this survey.

Do you know where you are going?

UNIT 19

This unit uses the context of the history of navigation to cover different ways of describing direction. It also encourages students to consider whom or what they trust when making decisions about the direction of their lives.

Using this unit

This unit could be used with all GCSE students and provides work on the different ways used to describe direction. The material is all found in the Foundation Tier but is suitable for Intermediate and Higher Tier students as well. Knowledge of angles is assumed, particularly that one revolution is 360°, that a straight line is 180° and that a right angle is 90°. The unit lasts for about 2 to 3 hours, depending on how many of the optional activities are used.

The students are introduced to three ways of describing direction that have been used in navigation. These are the 32 compass points, the quadrantal method and three figure bearings. There is a further section using scale drawing.

There are other activities, which encourage students to think about the experience of the early navigators and the trust that these people demonstrated in the compass. This is used as an analogy for finding our way in life. These tasks involve some discussion. This could be organised through a whole class discussion or small group work overseen by the teacher. It helps students to prepare for discussion if they are encouraged to write down their thoughts on the questions.

Mathematical content

Shape, space and measure (AT3)

- Understand and use the standard 32 compass points
- Understand and use the quadrantal methods
- Understand and use 3 figure bearings
- Use scale drawing to solve problems

Spiritual and moral development

The aim of the unit is to encourage students to reflect on how they trust in things, which they can not necessarily see or fully understand. It is hoped that by doing so they will deepen their understanding about the nature of faith.

Students will need a copy of a local map.
All students require a ruler and protractor.

TEACHER'S NOTES

Background

The history of navigation is full of examples of people who have travelled into the unknown with little to guide them. Sailors down the ages have chosen to trust the compass even when it was not fully understood.

Our lives are full of examples where we choose to trust in situations where we can not see. For some people, faith in God is related to this. A Christian understanding of faith is "being sure of what we hope for and certain of what we do not see" (Hebrews 11:1).

Notes on the Activities

Task 1:
This task should be done in pairs and will involve giving clear instructions and listening carefully. Students should then be encouraged to note down the directions of their partners.

Class discussion

Following the pair work, the class could discuss the following issues:

- The routes they chose,
- What sort of directions were used?
- How much did they rely on landmarks as fixed points?
- How would their sort of directions work at sea?

Tasks 2, 4, and 5:
Before beginning these tasks students may need more explanation on compass points, the quadrantal method and three figure bearings respectively. The tasks all rely on students having access to a map. Ideally, this should be a local map or a copy of a relevant part of it.

Task 3:
If angle work is weak then some preliminary revision may be required here, including the use of the protractor.

Losing your way

Students should first be encouraged to produce a written response, which can then inform a later whole class or group discussion.

Task 6:
Before beginning this task some students may need further explanation on how to interpret scales.

Having faith in the compass

The final activity encourages students to reflect on broader issues again. There are two key questions which students are asked to consider, both related to trust. They should be given time to consider these questions and to produce a written response before having a final class discussion.

Answers

Task 2:

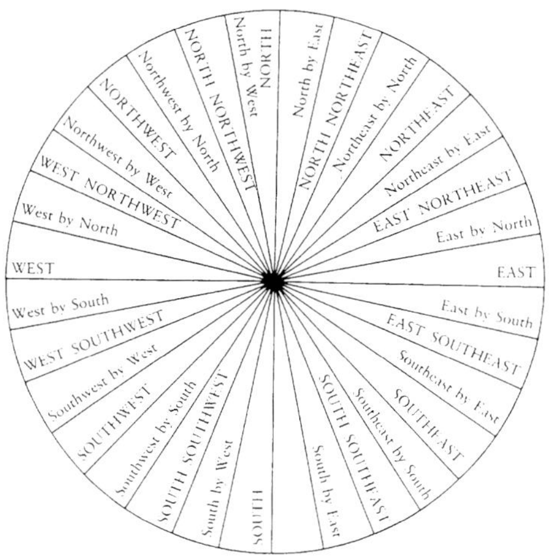

Task 3:

1. 90º, 2. 45º, 3. 22.5º, 4. 11.25º, 5. 90º, 6. 180º, 7. 123.75º, 8. 90º, 9. 135º, 10. 146.25º.

Task 4:

1. a) S45ºE, b) N45ºW, c) S45ºW, d) N45ºE, e) S11.25ºW, f) N22.5ºW, g) N33.75ºE.

2.

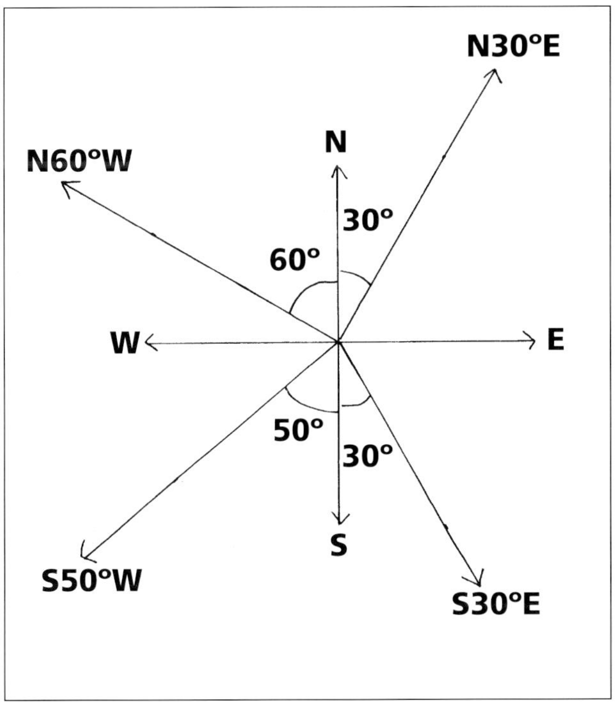

Task 5:

1. Because the compass needle points to north and so provides a fixed point.

2. a) 135º, b) 225º, c) 270º, d) 067.5º.

3. a) 030º, b) 130º, c) 280º, d) 195º.

Task 6:

1. a) 062º, b) 115º, c) 165º , d) 345º.

2. Distance: 5.76 miles; bearing: 101º.

3. Distance: 1.6 km; bearing: 332º.

TEACHER'S NOTES

Do you know where you are going?

UNIT 19

Throughout history people have been exploring more and more of our world. This means that they have always tried to improve their ways of navigating. In this unit, you are going to learn about some of the different ways which have been used in the past and which are still being used today for navigation. You will also spend some time thinking about what it is like to trust in something which you cannot see and do not fully understand.

1

This is a task for pairs. Choose two places in different parts of the school. Make up directions to take you from one place to the other. Then take it in turns to describe your routes to each other. You will need to give clear directions.

While you are listening to your partner's description, write down the following:

- where the journey starts and ends,
- the type of directions your partner uses,
- any fixed points that your partner refers to (e.g. the staff room).

The cardinal points

Early sailors used the stars as a navigation aid. They realised that certain stars appeared to stay in the same place in the sky. In the Northern Hemisphere, they used the North Star (also known as the Pole Star) as a fixed point to guide them in their navigation.

The problem with using stars for navigation was that they were only visible on clear nights. An alternative method was found when it was discovered that a particular kind of metal, when suspended freely, always pointed in the same direction and this direction was towards the North Star! This led to the invention of the compass. Once the direction north was defined, the directions east, south and west were easy to mark on the compass. These four directions are called the cardinal points of the compass.

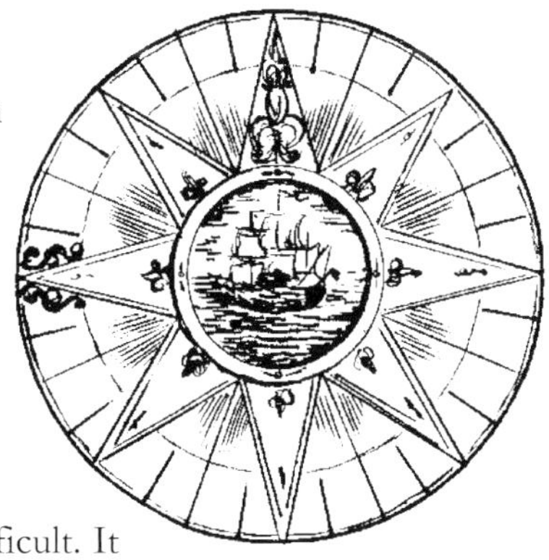

Steering a sailing boat is difficult. It is easiest to sail in the direction of a cardinal point. This is because it is easier to keep the needle of the compass on a well-defined point.

This meant, for example, that sailors navigating to the West Indies from England would sail southwards along the coasts of France and Spain until they reached the right distance north of the equator and then sail due west. (They knew how far south to go by the position of the sun.)

Going where no man has gone before

Put yourself in the position of the early explorers.

How would you feel going somewhere you had never been before and possibly where no one else had been either?

How would you feel depending on a compass that you did not really understand?

Boxing the compass

The first real development of the compass was to split the circle into 32 directions, all equally spaced. After marking the cardinal points on the circumference, each quadrant was split into half. Halfway between north and east was called north-east. Then these sections were split into half again. Halfway between north-east and north was defined as north-north-east. Halfway between north-north-east and north was defined as north by east. Finally, these new sections were split in half again. Naming the points round the compass is called "boxing the compass".

The full list of points for the first "quadrant" are, in order, North, North by East, North-North East, North-east by North, North-east, North-east by East, East-North East, East by North, East.

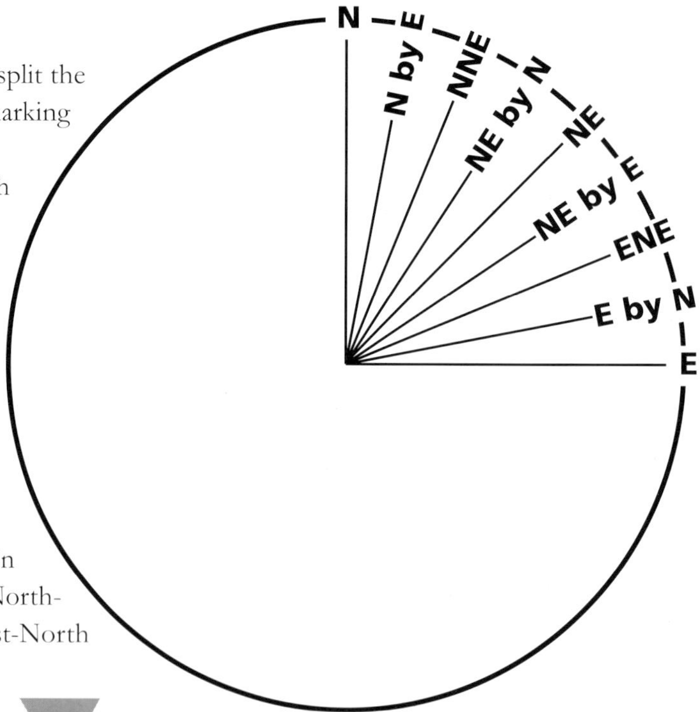

2

1. Copy the diagram and then box the compass for all 32 points.
2. Find a map of your local area including your school. Use compass points to write down the directions of five places from your school or from each other. (You might write, for instance, that the station is north-east of the school.)

The journey of life

Life is sometimes thought of as a journey. We need guidance and reference points in order to complete our journey of life satisfactorily.

Do you know where you are going in life?

How do you make decisions about the direction of your life?

Who guides you in your life journey? Parents, friends, God, teachers, ...?

360 degrees!

Boxing the compass was a relatively crude method of defining direction but in the earliest days of sailing it was not necessary to be more accurate because a boat could not be sailed to that degree of accuracy! As abilities increased, however, a more accurate method was necessary and the degree was defined. Rather than have just 32 divisions, the compass circle was split into 360 divisions.

3

For each of the following work out the angle between:

1. north and east,
2. north and north-east,
3. north and north-north-east,
4. north and north by east,
5. north by east and east by south,
6. east by south and west by north,
7. north-east and south by east,
8. west by north and north by east,
9. north-west and east,
10. south-west and east by north.

The quadrantal method

When degrees were first used to describe direction, sailors were not keen to give up the cardinal points and so a mixture was used. In this method the angle turned from north or south was given towards east or west.
For example:

70° east of north would be given as N70°E. (Note, this is not written E20°N)

50° west of south would be given as S50°W

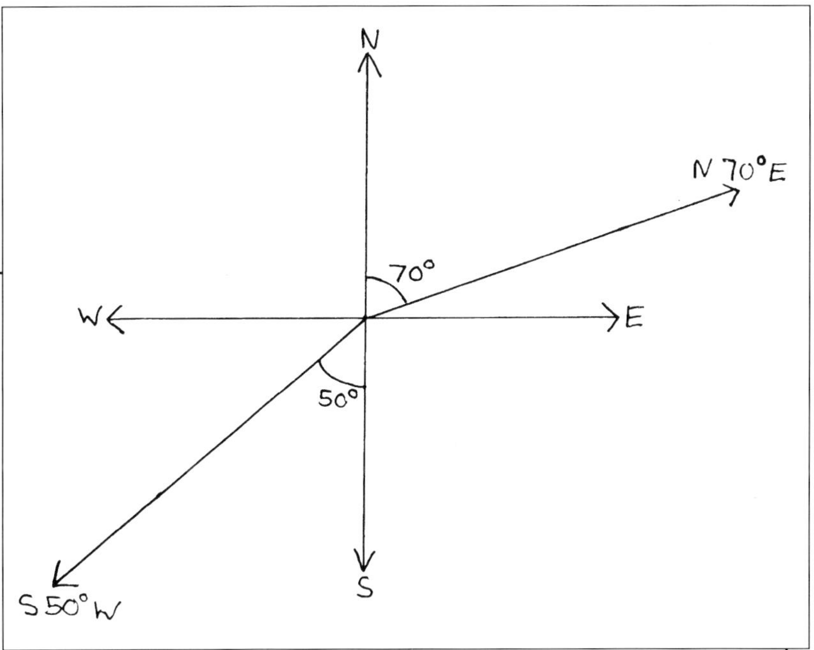

4

1. Write the following directions using the quadrantal method
   a) south-east
   b) north-west
   c) south-west
   d) north-east
   e) south by west
   f) north-north-west
   g) north-east by north

2. On a page draw some lines representing north-south and east-west, as shown here. Using your protractor and ruler draw lines representing the following directions.
   a) N30°E
   b) S30°E
   c) N60°W
   d) S50°W

3. Look again at the five directions you wrote for the places on your local map. Rewrite the statements using the quadrantal form. Are any of them more accurate using this method?

Three figure bearings

The main way now used to navigate is by using bearings. Like the quadrantal method, bearings are also given in degrees. The bearing is the clockwise angle between direction north and the direction you are describing. For example, for east the angle is 90° and for north-east it is 45°. So the angle can be anything from 0°to 360°. To avoid confusion the angle is always given as three digits, even if its size is less than 100°. So north will be given as 000° and north-east will be 045°. The sailor would read this as "zero four five degrees".

5

1. Why do you think north was chosen as the starting direction to measure bearings from?

2. Describe the following compass directions using three figure bearings:
   a) south-east
   b) south-west
   c) west
   d) east-north-east

3. Describe the following quadrantal method directions using three figure bearings:
   a) N30°E
   b) S50°E
   c) N80°W
   d) S15°W

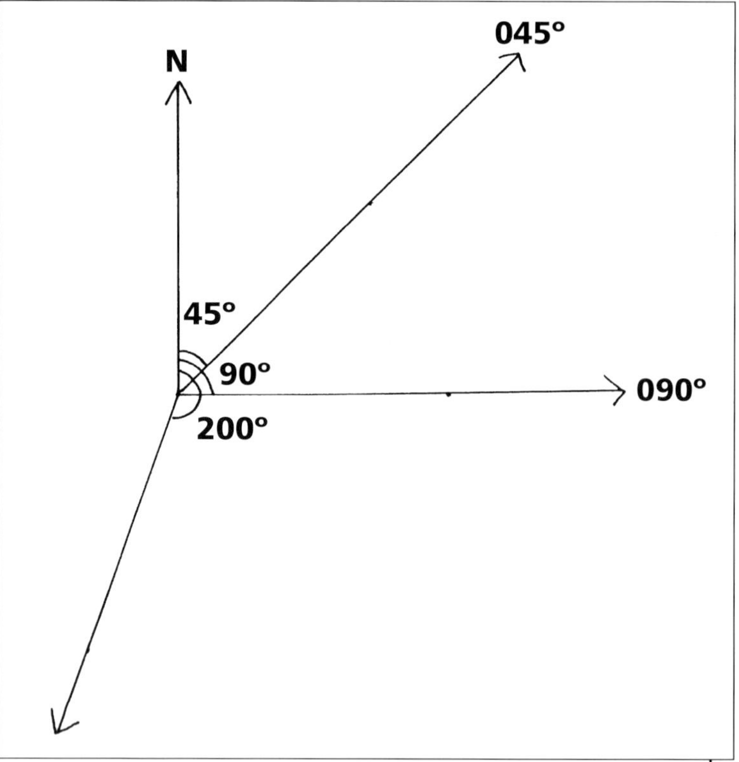

4. Look again at the five directions you wrote for the places on your local map. Write each of these using bearings.

Losing your way

Have you ever been lost?

What was the situation when you were lost?

How did it feel?

What did you do to "find yourself" again?

Write a few lines to answer these questions.

Scale Drawings

If you want to know the distance and bearing of places from other places you can measure them over the ground, or you can measure them on a map. A scale drawing is really just a simple map.

Scales are often written like this, 1: 5000. This means that one unit on paper represents 5000 units on the earth, whatever the unit. For example 1 cm represents 5000 cm or 50 metres.
Another way of writing the scale is 1 cm = 50 metres.

6

1. In the diagram find:
   a) the bearing of point B from point A,
   b) the bearing of point C from point A,
   c) the bearing of point C from point B,
   d) the bearing of point B from point C.

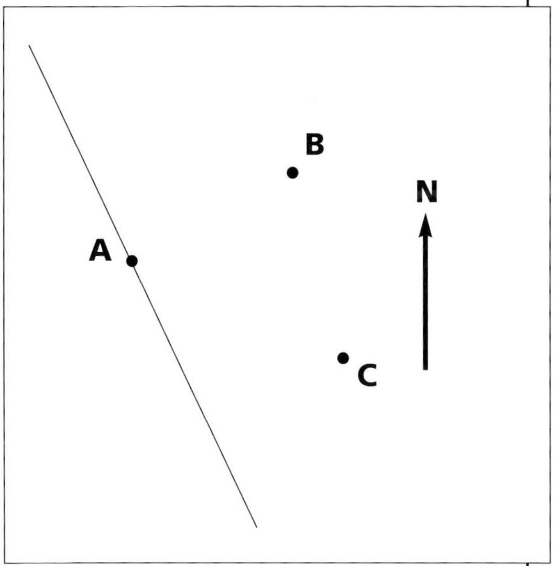

2. A ship leaves a port A and sails on a bearing of 060° for three miles. The captain then alters course so that the ship is sailing on a bearing of 130° for four miles. How far and on what bearing is the ship now from the port?

3. An orienteering course on a moor has these instructions:
   Stage 1: From the start travel 2 km on a bearing of 050° to point W.
   Stage 2: From point W travel 3 km on a bearing of 140° to point X.
   Stage 3: From point X travel 1 km on a bearing of 170° to point Y.
   Stage 4: From point Y travel 3 km on a bearing of 280° to point Z.
   Stage 5: From point Z return to the start.

   a) Mark the starting point (S) in the middle of a sheet of paper and indicate the direction north up the page
   b) Using a scale of 2 cm to represent 1 km, draw the orienteering course
   c) Give the bearing and distance for stage 5 so that the orienteer can get back from point D back to the starting point.

Having faith in the compass

A navigator on the seas or an orienteer on a moor both depend on the compass. The compass needle responds to the earth's invisible magnetic field. Although people can not see this field, they are prepared to trust in it as reliable.

Can you think of any other situation in which you are prepared to trust in something without seeing it?

As the compass responds to something unseen some people put their trust in an unseen God as they try to make sense of problems and attempt to make right decisions.

Who do you put your trust in when making your life decisions?